FAITH for the OLDER YEARS

FAITH for the OLDER YEARS

Making the Most of Life's Second Half

Paul B. Maves

AUGSBURG Publishing House • Minneapolis

FAITH FOR THE OLDER YEARS
Making the Most of Life's Second Half

Copyright © 1986 Augsburg Publishing House

Scripture quotations unless otherwise noted are from the Holy Bible: New International Version. Copyright 1978 by the New York International Bible Society. Used by permission of Zondervan Bible Publishers.

Library of Congress Cataloging-in-Publication Data

Maves, Paul B.
    FAITH FOR THE OLDER YEARS.

    Bibliography: p.
    1. Aged—Religious life.   I. Title.
BV4580.M36   1986   248.8'5   85-30716
ISBN 0-8066-2195-8

Manufactured in the U.S.A.   APH 10-2181

1   2   3   4   5   6   7   8   9   0   1   2   3   4   5   6   7   8   9

Contents

Preface

This book is an attempt to respond to questions put to me over the years by many persons. Also it is an attempt to clarify my own faith so as to chart my own course through time more faithfully. I am painfully aware that this is not the final answer to the questions posed. I only hope it will be the beginning of ongoing conversations. These conversations actually go back to a seminar that the late Carl Michalson—classmate, colleague, and friend—and I led together at Drew University Theological School in the early 1950s. Michalson's *Faith for Personal Crises* came out of this seminar. Carl constantly nudged me toward a sharper definition of my own theological understanding.

I am grateful to Therese Bremer, now a counselor in the Los Angeles area, and to Tom Cook, formerly Executive Director of the National Interfaith Coalition on Aging, who read some of my first attempts to put these thoughts into writing and encouraged me to go further. I am grateful to Robert W. McClellan of San Diego, whose friendship continues to give me confidence. I owe much to Elbert Cole, pastor of Central United Methodist Church in Kansas City, Missouri, who enabled me to participate in the National Shepherd's Center Project.

I am indebted to the Texas Conference of Churches, which invited me to reflect with them on a theology of aging in the summer of 1973; to the Rev. Howard Paul and the congregation of La Mesa Presbyterian Church in Albuquerque, who invited me to lecture on these topics; to two adult classes in Valley View United Methodist Church in Overland Park, Kansas, who allowed me to try out this material on them; and to my friend Howard Washburn, who has given distinguished leadership to ministry with the aging and enabled me to share in it.

Many persons have contributed: friends, parishioners, and residents of Kingsley Manor in Los Angeles who taught me by word and example how to live out the years with grace, humor, and dignity. I owe much to those who continue to nurture me by their caring. Most of all I am indebted to Mary Carolyn Maves—wife, companion, supporter, and critic—whose careful editorial work added polish to my communication.

Some of the names of persons referred to in this book have been changed in order to protect privacy.

CHAPTER ONE

New Images of Old Age

For almost 40 years I have been involved professionally in the study of aging and in ministry with older people, beginning when I was 33 years of age. My professional interest in aging began when I accepted a position as research associate in the Department of Pastoral Care in the then Federal Council of the Churches of Christ in America to do a two-year study of the church's ministry to older people. As a result of this study, in 1949 Lennart Cedarleaf and I published a book on *Older People and the Church*. In 1951 I wrote a pastoral-aid book entitled *The Best Is Yet to Be*.

Over the years I have read widely in the field, talked with many older people, worked with older people in camps, conferences, and in churches, and served as the administrator of a retirement home. During all this time, of course, I observed my own aging as well as that of others.

However, now that I am in my 70s, the experience of being old impinges on my consciousness with a special piquancy. I have seen the shadow of death passing down the hall just outside my door and know that it will not be too many years before we take a walk together. Now I can write about aging from the inside, as one who is there. The questions that many of my older friends and colleagues have raised have become the questions that I must answer now in a new way. I write to clarify my own thoughts about what it means and what I can do about it. In the process I hope to pull together what the years have taught me.

I was elected to senior citizenship at 63 when my wife and I went to the Norton Simon Museum of Art in Pasadena one Sunday afternoon to view the art displayed there. I walked up to the desk to pay $2.50 for admission. The young woman behind the desk looked up at me and said, "The Senior Citizens' tickets are 50 cents." I knew then that I was passing into later maturity. Since then ticket sellers at movie windows and gallery desks and public service buses automatically give me the reduced rate. In England my wife and I discovered that we were Old Age Pensioners rather than Senior Citizens.

On her 70th birthday, when she was what she called "safely old," May Sarton said, "I have always longed to be old, and that is because all my life I have had such great exemplars of old age, such marvelous models to contemplate."[1]

I too have had some beautiful and remarkable models of aging to contemplate and to emulate. However, I cannot say that I ever looked forward to becoming old with any eagerness. Now that I am here, there are many things about my life I enjoy and value that were not possible before. It is good not to feel under pressure to meet daily deadlines and not to have to achieve. It is good to know that I no longer need to gather and to save up for a rainy day. But I find it hard to accept the slowing down, the lessened energy, the eyes that tire much more quickly and demand trifocals, among other things.

For three years I was the administrator of a retirement home in Los Angeles. One day I met an attractive, well-dressed woman of 86 who was making her way slowly to the dining room. I greeted her. "How is everything going?"

She stopped and stood for a moment with both hands on her cane. "As well as can be expected, I guess." She paused. "This business of getting old is for the birds!" Then she smiled. "Of course, when I think about the alternative, I guess I'll take getting old. But I still think Shaw was right when he said youth was too good to be wasted on the young."

Probably most of us who are living in the last one-third of our lives would agree with her. Probably most of those under 60 view the prospect of old age with real dread when they let themselves think about it. All of us want to live a long time, but few of us want to get old. And if we must get old, we fervently hope we can be spared the vicissitudes of old age.

Throughout much of our history, in most of our literature, and generally in contemporary mass media, old age is depicted as a calamity. In discussions of public policy older people are thought of as problems. Older people are believed to be responsible for inflation, budgetary deficits, and a faltering economy, to say nothing of being a nuisance to those who are expected to care for them. Too many of us are too old. We live too long. We are a burden to care for. We remind the young of the fate that is facing them. Never mind that we are a whole new market for goods and services, the source of a new industry, and a possible reservoir for productive labor.

Ironically, much of this dread of old age and the negative bias against old people arises out of the prevailing image or stereotype, not out of the reality. The meaning of any event or situation, whether we look back in reflection or look ahead in anticipation, is determined by what we have been taught to see or expect to see as much as by what is really there. This determines how we feel and what we do about the situation. Our expectations tend to become self-fulfilling prophecies.

Each of us can look at the same set of data and perceive it differently. A woman and her two small daughters planted a bush in the garden. Some time later one came in holding her hand and crying, "Your rose bush has stickers on it." Then the other came in. "Oh, Mommy, our thorn bush is all covered with roses."

Think of the word *old*. By itself it may conjure up images of precious heirlooms or handmade antiques, or "old masters" works of art. You may think of rare old wine, aged cheese, ancient monuments like the Parthenon in Athens or the pyramids in Egypt. You may even recall the beauty of a gnarled tree stubbornly clinging to the hilltop where it has wrestled with the wind over many years and won. In contrast, *old man, old woman* may bring up unpleasant or disgusting associations. Wrinkles, sickness, weakness, forgetfulness, uselessness, crotchetiness, loneliness, nursing homes, incontinence may come to mind.

Now think for a moment about some old people who may have been important in your life. I suspect you could name some who fit the stereotype, but even more who do not. If they do not fit the stereotype, you may not have thought of them as being old. The image we hold of later maturity not only shapes our attitude but also affects our behavior.

So over against the all-too-prevalent view of old age as a time of suffering and loss I want to place the view of old age as a time of increasing satisfaction in living. Over against the view of older people as problems I want to pose the view that they constitute one of our most valuable social resources.

Contrasting Views of Old Age

Both views can be found in the Bible. One of the most beautiful but most pessimistic descriptions of old age in all literature is in Eccles. 11:8-12. The message of the Preacher there is that we should rejoice in our youth, for evil days lie ahead. Even if we can celebrate many years, we do so knowing that darkness lies beyond.

This view, if not influenced by the common Greek outlook, is at least akin to it. In his book *The View in Winter* Ronald Blythe reviews the Greek attitude to old age based on their idealization of youth and physical beauty or perfection, so that Meander could write "Whom the gods love die young," and Plautus could see early death as a divine favor.[2]

In the Old Testament the white hair of old age is called a crown of glory. A long life is seen as the reward for righteousness. Respect for fathers and mothers is enjoined as the recipe for survival as a nation. Paul wrote his second letter to the Corinthians when he was an old man by the standards of his time, having survived a strenuous life marked by hardship, persecution, shipwreck, pain, and rejection. He wrote:

> We have this treasure [our vocation to ministry] in jars of clay to show that this all-surpassing power is from God and not from us. . . Though outwardly we are wasting away, yet inwardly we are being renewed day by day. For our light and momentary troubles are achieving for us an eternal glory that far outweighs them all. So we fix our eyes not on what is seen, but on what is unseen. For what is seen is temporary, but what is unseen is eternal (2 Cor. 4:7, 16b-18).

Much earlier, even among the Greeks, Plato challenged the worship of physical perfection and located beauty in the spirit, which he saw as eternal, rather than in the transient flesh.

Granted, a visit to a nursing home can present one with illustrations of the hazards faced in old age. We may even look at the 10% of the elderly who are homebound. We can base our image of old age upon the 20% who in varying degrees can be described as casualties of the aging process, or we can base it on the 80% who are numbered among the survivors and the enjoyers. And even within the nursing home itself, where five percent of the older population live, it is possible to find illustrations of gallantry in facing the darkness, courage in enduring suffering, and creativity in coping. Even there among some the fires of life glow warmly, and hope marvels at the rainbow.

A long life does present problems. It also holds possibilities. Some of these possibilities are available only to those who have lived a long time. If you are fortunate enough to have lived 70 years, remember that about half of those born the same time you were have already died.

No age is a time of unmitigated triumph or unending bliss. No age has a monopoly on satisfaction or on freedom from suffering or loss. In fact chronological age plays only a small part in defining who we are or in determining how we are. In the 1975 Louis Harris poll, while 45% of those 65 and over thought life could be better, an even higher 49% of those under 65 felt the same way. One in three older persons said they were pleasantly surprised with the way their later years had turned out.[3]

A New Image of Old Age

So I dare to make the following affirmations, which in part are articles of faith, but which in a large part are based on research data, and which are generalizations about old age without being descriptions of the experience of any one person.

1. Old age can be as satisfying as any age

The last one-third of life can be as satisfying, as meaningful, and as fulfilling as any other period of life, in spite of any pain or loss we may sustain. As the consummation and the completion of life, the last one-third ought to be more meaningful than any other period of life. In making this affirmation let me lay to rest some of the stereotypes held by so many.

Not a time of disability

For most of us later maturity is not a time of sickness or disability. Sixty-nine percent of us report that our health is excellent or good. Eighty-five percent of us are functionally healthy, that is to say, we can do whatever we want to do provided we are willing to modify our expectations somewhat and make use of some prosthetic props. We may no longer run in marathons, although some of us do, but we can walk long distances, and even with artificial joints some of us jog. We may have to wear glasses and use stronger light; we may have to wear hearing aids and sit up front; but what we look for and what we listen to is more important than the fact that we can see and hear. Unfortunately, some of us resist wearing glasses, using bifocals, putting on hearing aids, or carrying a cane because of vanity or fear of being devalued as old, or we attempt to deny the reality of the changes we are experiencing. As a result we handicap ourselves unnecessarily. It is true that 80% of us have some chronic physical disability that bothers us, but many of these disabilities were incurred when we were much younger, and we may have lived with them for a long time.

While health is a primary concern for most of us, we are learning that we have to distinguish between the aging process and disease. Disease is not an integral aspect of growing older, any more than it is inevitable. Many of the chronic, degenerative diseases from which people are dying now are preventable, postponable, or treatable, and often are rooted in life-styles. Through proper diet, adequate exercise and rest, control of obesity, avoidance of drug misuse or abuse, and refraining from overindulgence in alcoholic beverages, from smoking, and other toxins, many of our chronic degenerative diseases can be prevented. Even such a simple practice as fastening seat belts could prevent numberless cases of disability acquired in automobile accidents.

In some ways living is like running through a field that has been mined. The longer we go on, the more likely we are to detonate a mine. Some of us will encounter the mine on the first steps into the field. Others of us will get all the way through unscathed.

Some of us worry more about becoming senile and losing our minds. First let me say that we ought to quit using the term *senile*. Originally it simply meant "old" and is related to the words *senior* and *senator*. Then, because we thought old age was a disease, *senility* came to mean "a disease," which was then brushed off as inevitable, irreversible, and untreatable. Anything that was not understood or easily diagnosed was labeled "senile" and pushed away. We are learning now to talk about specific diseases and to diagnose organic brain damage from disease.

Only about 10% of us will experience any serious organic brain damage that affects our mental functioning. We are finding that many of the dementias or loss of mental functioning that have been blamed on aging are really the results of such things as malnutrition, operable tumors, drug misuse or abuse, depression, boredom, environmental toxins, or a life without hope. Many of these causes of mental loss can be eradicated. Many more can be prevented.

Not a time of poverty

To turn to another stereotype, later maturity is not necessarily a time of poverty. It is true that during the time of the Great Depression of the 1930s, when the Social Security program was initiated, more than half of all older people were reduced to poverty as defined by federal standards. But in recent years surveys and census reports indicate that only about 15% of those 65 and older live below the poverty level. Even if we raise the level to 125% of the official standard, only a fifth or a fourth of all older people are poor.

But this is about the same figure as for all other age groups, although a slightly larger percentage of children than older adults live in poverty—to our shame. Most of the elderly poor have been poor all their lives. Most of the elderly poor are found among ethnic minority groups. Most are single women. So to a large extent poverty in old age is rooted in the poverty endemic to our society. It is caused by social policies that put women at an economic disadvantage and by the way in which we provide health care, because a serious illness, a long hospitalization, or many months in a nursing home can soon pauperize one with limited health insurance, a fixed income, and small savings.

There are homeless men and women who roam our streets and sleep under bridges or doorways or occupy single rooms in dilapidated hotels. Older people can be found living in squalor. We need to be concerned about them. But the point here is that we do not base our image of old age or our expectation on this minority alone.

Another point is that we need to give more attention to financial planning, to estate planning, and to the development of social policies that alleviate the unemployment, the underemployment, and the handicapping conditions that militate against the maintenance of an adequate income in the later years.

Not a time of loneliness

Contrary to still another stereotype, for most of us old age is not a time of loneliness and neglect. Only 13% of us admit to being lonely, contrary to what 65% of young people believe about us. Much has been made of the abandonment of older people by their families. But the reality is that most older people live near relatives and see at least one child once a week.

Others, whose children are scattered, keep in touch by letter and telephone. The family is no longer an economic unit able to be fully responsible for financial support or for nursing care, but it is a very important psychological support.

It is true that most older people do not live with their children and prefer it that way, although they value their relationship with their children. It is true that about 5% of older people are in nursing homes. But even there families visit, and some studies have shown that relations between children and parents improve when the parent moves to a nursing home after the physical burden of care has become intolerable. We must keep in mind that about 70% of those in nursing homes are women, mostly widows, and that 50% of them have no families to care for them. To balance the picture we need to remember that about 85% of the care to older people is given by the informal support networks of family, neighbors, and friends.

Churches, clubs, senior centers, support groups, and college and university programs all provide opportunities for us to maintain social contacts and to make new friends. We do need to be concerned about that group in the older population who are homebound. However, even homebound persons can take some initiative to maintain relations by using the telephone, writing letters, and entertaining visitors. Those in need, however, do not define for us our prevailing image of old age.

2. Old age can be a time of continued learning

The last one-third of our lives can be a time of continuing personal and spiritual growth. It need not be a time of stagnation or the ossification of our mental faculties. Our minds do not necessarily deteriorate, and our IQs do not fall as we age, except as we let them atrophy from disuse.

We do not inevitably lose our memory

Contrary to another stereotype, we do not necessarily become more forgetful as we grow older. Young people forget too, but they do not worry about it. When we get past 30 and forget something, we tend to blame it on getting older. The worry induced by the myth of senile deterioration itself interferes with memory. One difference as we grow older is that we accumulate so much more data to be stored in our memory that it takes longer to process it. As we move from one setting to another, the mental indices that could trigger the memory get buried. Still another difference is that as we become jaded with experience, we do not pay attention to what we encounter and make no effort to fix the impression in our minds. In other words, we have learned to practice selective inattention, assuming that we will have no need to recall what is being presented to us, for instance, when we are introduced to new persons. Again, fatigue, illness, drugs, boredom, and depression do interfere with memory.

We can learn

For a long time there has been a cliche that one cannot teach new tricks to an old dog. But older people can and do learn. There are those among us who are learning new languages, learning to type or to use computers and calculators, mastering new games, learning to play musical instruments, and acquiring new artistic skills. Some of us are enrolling in college classes and securing degrees. We are taking up painting and weaving. We are reading and attending lectures to keep us abreast of current events.

In the 1961 White House Conference on Aging, Rabbi Abraham J. Heschel, then president of the Hebrew Union Theological Seminary in New York, said:

> May I suggest that man's potential for change and growth is much greater than we are willing to admit. . . .

The years of old age may enable us to attain the high values we failed to sense, the insights we have missed, the wisdom we have ignored. . . .

One ought to enter old age the way one enters the senior year at the university, in exciting anticipation of the summing up and consummation.[4]

We need to remind ourselves that wisdom does not accrue to us automatically as we grow older. Aging can accentuate our stupidity and deepen our prejudices and lock us more firmly into disfunctional values and behavior unless we commit ourselves to learn and open ourselves to new experiences that provide new information. As we grow older, we may become more skilled at insulating ourselves from new information as a way of keeping from being disturbed, until we get completely out of touch with reality.

In the later years we need to continue to learn in order to keep abreast of a changing world and to cope with changing circumstances. We need to learn in order to add color and spice to our daily routines. We need to learn in order to continue to be desirable to have around, to be fun to live with, to be interesting companions and valuable fellow sojourners along the way.

3. Old age can be a time of continued creativity

Later maturity can be a time for continued creativity and productivity and for the breaking of new ground for generations yet to come. We can continue to participate in the creation of the world in which we live. We can shape the culture we will leave behind us and enrich our heritage.

A woman who for years had a hobby of decorating cakes for special occasions took her first painting lesson at the age of 86. At the age of 94, although now using a wheelchair, she is still painting and selling her paintings to persons all over the metropolitan area. A man secured his Ph.D. degree in his 70s. Others are writing poetry, constructing plays, creating fiction, putting their memoirs together as a gift to their children. Some are contributing to the oral history of their time and place. Representatives, senators, judges, and even a president are demonstrating that in their later years they can continue to provide significant leadership to the nation.

In his book *The Ulyssean Adult* John A. B. MacLeish musters evidence that creativity is not only possible but ought to be normative in the middle and later years.[5] He cites case after case in which persons have made significant creative contributions in their 70s and 80s, refuting the assumption of many, and the research of some, that only the young are creative.

Of course, productivity and creativity function on many levels. They need not be spectacular nor widely acclaimed to be important. Many of us who are unknown and unsung are quietly going about our daily business and making important contributions to our families, our communities, and the organizations to which we belong, making life richer for all who come into contact with us.

About 13% of those 65 and over choose to remain in the labor force, either working or looking for work, full or part-time. Others would continue to work or return to work if encouraged to do so or if arrangements were made for them to work part-time or on a flexible schedule. Many who have retired from gainful employment have filled their days with volunteer work in the community, contributing service which if it had to be paid for would amount to billions of dollars. Others devote time and energy to the care of relatives, including children and grandchildren. Many are supporting other persons and worthy causes with financial gifts.

Most older people want to be useful. They do not relish the prospect of being laid on the shelf or of being a burden on others. Society must learn how to tap this reservoir of time, talent, and training. Older people themselves must become more active in finding ways to put their experience, knowledge, and skill at the disposal of the community.

You may object that this image of old age is too optimistic, perhaps even romantic, out of touch with the tragedy that pervades human existence. You may believe it to be blind to the suffering of those who stumble and fall along the way. Optimistic, yes. But it is an optimism based on a faith in the possibility of transcending adversity. It is based on the vision of a Spirit moving over chaos to create a universe and of a love that is drawing persons into unity. It is confirmed by the observation that many are achieving such a graceful old age and dying with dignity and honor.

In my early 70s I am well aware that my body will not do all the things it could do when I was 17. I experience more pain now than in those early years. It takes me longer to recover from illness than it once did. There has been some diminishment in my sensory capacities. I am well aware that in spite of all the caution I can exert I could be involved in an accident that would leave me crippled. I could experience a painful and disabling disease. I could suffer the loss of persons I love and depend on for the confirmation of my worth as a person. But this has been true for all of my life. These are the hazards we face by being alive, not from getting older.

At the same time I rejoice because I have been allowed to live so long when many of my contemporaries are already dead and to be so healthy when many my age have long since experienced serious debility. Those of us who have reached 70 are the lucky ones. We are the survivors.

The fact that old age is possible now for the majority of us for the first time in human history is a magnificent achievement, something to be celebrated. More than 25 years have been added to life expectancy in this century. At the same time the possibilities for living fruitfully have been multiplied. Now that later maturity is given to us as a gift, let us take advantage of it and learn how to live fully in these extra years.

Remember, too, that we are living in a new age. Those of us who are old today not only are more numerous than those of a generation ago, but also we are different. We are better educated. We are healthier. We are more at home in a complex, urbanized, technological society. We have more coping skills. We have more resources to draw on to keep us well and functioning effectively than any other generation has ever had.

I have discovered some real benefits from becoming elderly and from retirement. All my life I was driven by a need to make something of myself and to become "somebody." Now I am being freed from these drives by the realization I always was "somebody" and by the fact there are no more stairs available for me to climb in my upward striving. All my life I was driven by a dread of financial insecurity. Fortunately, because my pensions and savings are adequate to sustain me and my family, I am free from this. Also in the early years of my life I worried about being valued by others. Now I realize that it is more important to value others, and I am now aware that along the way I have been greatly loved.

Later Maturity Defined

What do we mean by later maturity? When do we become old? When do we enter old age? Who is an older adult? Do you consider yourself to be old? When do you think you will get old?

Most older people do not consider themselves to be old, because they think of old age as a condition of disability, although they will admit to being an older adult. Old age is ten years beyond where they are. They say you are as old as you feel or as old as you think you are or as old as you act. This makes old age a subjective condition that is unwanted or a social role that is not desired.

A person who is known to be retired, to live in a retirement community, or who is disabled probably will be defined as old by young people. However, it is hard to think of Bob Hope as old, because he is so active, even though he is 80. George Burns is known to be old, because he capitalizes on his age and is adored for what he makes of it.

The age of 65 was arbitrarily set as the age at which pensions could be collected and then as the age when retirement was made mandatory. It is sometimes said that this age was set in Germany by Otto Von Bismarck in the late 19th century, when few persons lived that long. Now some are suggesting that old age, and pension rights should not begin until 70.

Neither subjective judgments nor chronological age are very helpful as descriptions of a category of being. But for the purposes of reflecting on the later years of our lives and for developing ministries by, with, and for older people, I prefer to think of later maturity as the last one-third of our lives. For many of us this will be a span of 30 years or more. So allowing for great flexibility and for a five-year overlap between age groupings, I believe we should consider anyone over the age of 55 to be an older adult.

For most of us, the decade from 55 to 64 is one of *anticipation* and, it is to be hoped, *preparation* for retirement. It is a decade in which many of us will take early retirement or enter on a second career, full or part-time. It is a decade in which many of us lose our parents and the nest is emptied of children. For all of us the age of passage will be marked by birthdays, for some by outstanding events, for others by losses and changes.

Of course, for each of us the experience of aging will be different: some of us will retire at age 52, and some of us will die in harness at age 97, while most of us will fall somewhere in between. Some of us will be slowed by diminished physical capacity, while others of us will remain vigorous until the very end. Some of us will have resigned ourselves to the expected stereotypical role of being old, while others of us will go on learning and experimenting and enjoying life day by day.

How Long Will We Live?

This raises the question of how long we can expect to live. How long do you believe that you will live? On what do you base your estimate of the time left to you?

In 1983 the life expectancy at birth of Americans had risen to 74.6 years, compared with 49.4 in 1900, thus adding a quarter of a century to life expectancy in this century. Women live longer than men. A woman's life expectancy is 78.9 years, while that of a man is 70.9 years.[6] Life expectancy for any one group is related to economic circumstances, life-styles, the hazards of occupations, and access to medical care. Ethnic minorities do not anticipate as many years as white Americans; whites can be expected to live 6.1 years longer on the average than blacks. Studies indicate that the lower expectancy among men is caused by the use of tobacco, among other things.

Those of us who reach age 65 have a life expectancy of about 16 more years—again, longer for women and shorter for men. At any rate, when we turn 65, we still have a block of years stretching ahead to use as we will. A friend of mine says that when he reached the age of 70, he figured he had lived his life—the promised three score and ten; each year since then is a gift, the icing on the cake.

What Is the Human Life Span?

In spite of tremendous gains in average life expectancy in industrialized nations, the life span itself has not been notably extended. There have always been a few hardy and lucky individuals who have lived to a great age. We have simply made it possible now for more of us to come closer to living out our life span. There have been some extravagant claims that we can live to be 150 years of age, and there have been reports of areas of the world where many persons live to the age of 100 or more, because of diet or life-style. What are the limits of human life? We say "limits" because almost no one disputes the observation that the aging process in every species ends inevitably in death.

James F. Fries and Laurence Crapo have made a careful study of this question, published in their book *Vitality and Aging*.[7] They note that the oldest human being whose age could be documented beyond question lived to be 114. They concluded that the median life span had been for thousands of years and would continue to be 85 on the average.

Implications

What we can make of all this is that *life itself is a gift*. The years of old age given to us in this century are a bonus for us to use. In the long run it is not the length of life that counts, but the quality of our life. We are called to be stewards of this time and our talents. We can assume some responsibility for the kind of life that we will have in spite of all the challenges that are thrown at us. Life does not end at 40, or at 55, or at 65, or even 75. Possibility does not cease at any of these ages either.

Alfred Lord Tennyson drew on the legend of Ulysses for a hopeful image of the later years. The Greek story ends with Ulysses coming home from the Trojan wars after a long struggle and settling down. Tennyson imagines that the old warrior would not long be content to sit and rock, and so he hears Ulysses say these words to his old comrades in arms:

> Yet all experience is an arch wherethrough
> Gleams that untravell'd world, whose margin fades
> For ever and for ever when I move.
> How dull it is to pause, to make an end,
> To rust unburnish'd, not to shine in use!
> . . . .
> Old age hath yet his honour and his toil;
> Death closes all: but something ere the end,
> Some work of noble note, may yet be done,
> Not becoming men that strove with Gods.
> The lights begin to twinkle from the rocks:
> The long day wanes: the slow moon climbs: the deep
> Moans round with many voices. Come, my friends,
> 'Tis not too late to seek a newer world.
> Push off, and sitting well in order smite
> The sounding furrows; for my purpose holds
> To sail beyond the sunset, and the baths
> Of all the western stars, until I die.
> . . . .
> Though much is taken, much abides; and though
> We are not now that strength which in old days
> Moved earth and heaven; that which we are, we are;
> One equal temper of heroic hearts,
> Made weak by time and fate, but strong in will
> To strive, to seek, to find, and not to yield.[8]

Although Tennyson wrote this when he was only 31, he lived to be 83, and he maintained his optimistic outlook until the end. While this represents a masculine perspective, women too can continue to seek and to create a "newer world."

CHAPTER TWO

Living through Transitions

Every once in a while something happens to remind us that time is passing by and that we are getting older, whether we like it or not. Birthdays do that. For some of my friends the 40th birthday was especially traumatic, because it brought to mind such cliches as "over the hill" or "halfway through." Looking in the mirror and seeing some gray hair does that, or for men, watching the hairline recede. Maybe we begin to think, "I am no longer attractive," or, "My chances for getting another job are fewer."

If I recall correctly, turning 40 was no problem for me other than learning that I would need bifocals. When I reached 65, my reaction was one of disbelief, because I felt no different from what I had been at 40. But it did raise the question of whether I wanted to keep on working where I was or to retire and take it easy.

If we are professional athletes or if we prize speed and strength, waning reaction time may mean that our career in that field is coming to an end, or we may have to give up a valued activity. If we wake up in the morning with a twinge of rheumatism, we may wonder how we will get our work done that day. Perhaps we suddenly recall our mortality and think, "My time is running out."

To live is to age. To live a long time is to become old. Aging begins at birth and continues throughout the entire life span. But for the first 20 or 30 years of our lives the processes of growth and development mask the processes of aging. After we reach adulthood, aging becomes the dominant process, and in middle age we become especially conscious of it. In every living being the aging process culminates inevitably in death.

So to think about the process of aging is to raise the question of the meaning and purpose of the life which is loaned to us for a relatively brief span of years. The awareness of our own death distinguishes us from all other living creatures. This awareness underlies the development of religion, art, and philosophy. It fuels the concern for the quality of life and how best to use the time we have.

Why Do We Age and Die?

So it is natural to raise the question, Why do we grow old and die? This question is posed on two levels. On one level it is curiosity about the causes of aging as a natural process and a concern to trace accurately its trajectory. This is the level of science. On another level it is wonder about the meaning of aging, and about what the Creator had in mind by making aging and dying a part of the life process. This is the level of art, religion, theology, and philosophy; this is the province of the humanities. So let us look for a time at the aging process descriptively. Then let us look at it in terms of what it may mean for us personally.

Two caveats to keep in mind

1. Each of us is unique

Before we launch into a normative description of the aging process, we need to remind ourselves that the older we get the more we become unlike anyone else. The very real, but not very noticeable, differences that exist between us when we are born become accentuated through the years. To put it another way, the older we become, the more individuated we are. We are what we have always been—only more so—plus the effect of different experiences.

There are differences in the way the aging process develops within our own bodies, although there is a tendency in society to treat everyone of the same age alike. All five year olds are expected to go to school regardless of how they have developed, for example. So the age-graded expectation of how to behave again masks some of the real differences.

Then, too, different generations of persons experience different kinds of historical and cultural events. My generation, for instance, grew up in the midst of the Great Depression, which left its mark on most of us in one way or another.

Finally, each of us experiences events that are unique to us, whether in terms of relationships or opportunities or accidents, and each of us responds to similar events differently. The experience of marriage or of the Great Depression was different for each of us.

The point of all this is that it is hard to generalize about older adults. While we can make general statements about the aging process and how it affects persons, real understanding requires that we describe ourselves in terms of our life histories. We truly know each other only as we learn each other's stories. We come to understand ourselves finally only in terms of the story we tell to others.

2. We do not die of old age alone

The process of living exposes us to accidents that reduce our functioning capacity, to diseases that leave their own scars, to strains of various kinds that cause permanent injury. It is not only the biological process going on within but also the effects of our interaction with our environments that mark and change us. Sometimes it is hard to tell which is the most significant.

In the words of Albert Lansing, aging can be defined as

. . . a process of unfavorable progressive change, usually correlated with the passage of time, becoming apparent after maturity and terminating inevitably in the death of the individual. . . [It is] a process involving progressive loss of the ability to live.[1]

In this sense all of us are terminal cases living toward dying.

The individual of the species is expected to fend off the inroads of the environment long enough to come to maturity so it can reproduce itself. Human beings also have the responsibility not only to reproduce ourselves or at least contribute to the nurture of the young, but also to conserve, enrich, and transmit the accumulated cultural heritage of humankind. In this way we fulfill our human destiny, and having fulfilled our destiny, it is time to die.

In discussing the question of whether or not aging is a disease, H. Tristram Engelhardt Jr. points out that a disease is something that violates some expectations for the human condition. Disease might be defined as

a physical and/or psychological state of affairs held to be disteleological (for example, arthritis, circumscribing one's ability to be active), deforming (for example, vitiligo), or causing pain.[2]

To speak of aging as a disease is to say it is improper. If losses that attend aging could be prevented, such losses are diseases.

To call aging a disease puts older people in the sick role, recruits the medical profession and biomedical sciences to mark it out as their domain, labels it as improper, encourages people to refuse to accept it, and enlists individual responsibility to avoid it. Thus we may be led to believe that by the use of vitamins or certain kinds of skin creams old age itself can be avoided.

It is important to distinguish between aging and disease, because while aging itself is inevitable, disease processes can be guarded against or treated. Furthermore, it is important to make clear that the things about later maturity most of us fear are not related to chronology and can occur at any time in life. This point is illustrated by the fact that the diseases we die of today are different from those of a generation or two ago. In 1900 influenza and pneumonia ranked number one, while tuberculosis ranked number two. These have now been reduced by medical advances so that tuberculosis has almost been eradicated as a cause of death. Now we are dying of diseases of the heart and of cancer and other neoplasms. In other words, we used to die of the diseases more characteristic of the younger years, and now we die of diseases more likely to strike in the later years. We used to die of infectious diseases, and now we die of the degenerative diseases. But they are still diseases. While the infectious diseases struck out of the environment, the degenerative diseases tend to be brought on by the way we live.

The aging process described

So to age is to experience a succession of changes— changes in the body, changes in our way of thinking, changes in society and culture, and changes in the physical environment. *Gerontology* is the study of the changes persons undergo over time.

The biological process of aging is imperfectly understood.

Different theories account for it, with the question being not so much which theory is correct as which theory accounts for most of the changes. Some theories emphasize inherent, genetically determined alterations in multiplying cells that place a limit on the number of times they can multiply and rejuvenate themselves. Other theories speak of the degeneration of the nonmultiplying cells from exhaustion, depletion of inner reserves, and the accumulation of harmful substances within. Other theories point to the increase in scar tissue and the deterioration of connective tissues that interfere with the functioning of the organism. This suggests we wear out. Still others point to changes brought on by atrophy or disuse. This is in line with the folk wisdom that we rust out.

Any or all of these together result in characteristic or normal changes within us as we get older. One change is a reduction in reaction time. Another is an increasing length of time to recover from illness or accident. Another is an increase in fat compared to muscle. Another is a reduction in the amount of air expired by the lungs and the amount of blood pumped by the heart while resting. Another is a change in the hormonal secretion, causing a diminution of the sex drive. Perhaps the most noticeable biological change is a diminution of acuteness of sensory capacity. We may not see or hear as well. The lens of the eye tends to become yellower and more opaque, which causes us to need more light. The tissues of the eye become less flexible; this causes us to need more time to adjust from dark to light or to focus from near to far. Hearing may gradually diminish because of tissue and nerve changes, but also because of diseases or because of damage caused by excessive noise in the environment over a period of time.

In addition to these changes in our bodies, we also experience changes in our relationships with others. Relationships may be broken off by conflict. Loved ones may die or move away and drop out of touch. The community may change as the composition of the population changes.

Also we live through changes in our cultural environment, such as significant shifts in values and in what is socially acceptable. Daniel Yankelovich in his book *New Rules* documents the shift in values observable in the opinion polls he has taken over the last 30 years.[3] He likens the shift in values to the shift in the earth's crust that causes earthquakes. He describes this as a shift from an ethic of self-denial to one of self-fulfillment.

We may have to cope with changes in our physical environment as the open countryside of the pioneering community with its clean air gives way to the industrialized city with polluted air, as we shift from the use of trains to airplanes.

But more important than these changes—whether they be biological, social, or cultural—is the meaning of these changes for us and what we do with them. To live is to change.

We have here no continuing city

The author of the letter to the Hebrews wrote to second- and third-generation Christians whose religious problem was not unbelief but complacency. They had settled into a rut. They resisted innovation. They did not want to take chances. They were no longer aflame with enthusiasm to share the good news. They took security for granted. The writer wanted to stir them up to renew their zeal and to recover the excitement of the original congregation. So he reached back into their history, to the time when their forebears were nomads wandering over the desert, to call up an image of the Christian life as one of transiency and pilgrimage and search. He reminded them that they were only sojourners here. They were passing through. They were living in tents, likely to pull up stakes any day and move on. They had here no lasting city. So they were to seek the city whose builder and maker is God, a city with solid foundations that will not crumble and change.

You and I, too, live in a time when the world seems to seethe with change that shakes our self-identity and our sense of self-worth. Those of us who have lived more than 50 years have seen more changes than generations of those who lived before. Not only are we survivors; we have demonstrated our capacity to cope with change.

Dealing with change is not a new task for humankind. Five centuries before Christ, the Greek philosopher Heraclitus came to the conclusion that change was the one basic fact of existence to be reckoned with.

In a contemporary book called *Loss and Change* Peter Marris takes up the same theme based upon his observations of personal and social change in several different cultures.[4] He finds three categories of change.

1. There is *incremental* change, which takes place so gradually, so incidentally, that it is almost imperceptible. Usually we assimilate such change without being very aware of it. We buy a new house. We get a new car. We buy some new clothes in the latest fashion. We change our hairstyle. We look in the mirror every morning and see essentially what we saw when we were 16 until we go to a 25th class reunion and notice how everyone else has changed. Then we compare what we see in the mirror with the picture of the graduating class.

2. There is *growthful* change, which is welcomed and sought out, because we believe that the new will be better than the old. We complete a course of training to qualify for a better job. We get married in order to have companionship. We look forward to having children. We are promoted. We change careers in response to new opportunities looking for a better fit between our interests and our occupation.

3. But there also is *catastrophic* change, which usually is so traumatic or comes on us so suddenly that we are unprepared

for it. It demolishes the structures and the relationships that give meaning and stability to our lives. We lose our health. We are bereaved of a spouse. We suffer desertion or go through a divorce. Our business fails. Fires, floods, droughts, and devastation left by war may sweep away the work of a lifetime and with it our dreams.

Peter Marris points out that no matter how gradual, how welcome, or how growthful, every change is accompanied by some loss. If it does not cause pain, at least it demands additional energy and for a time causes confusion. In order to feel comfortable we need to keep our world stable so we know where we are, what we can count on, and how we should respond. All of us tend to resist change beyond a certain point. At the same time, we need the stimulation and the challenge that change brings, and we seek change because of the hope of being better off. So even if we are not devastated with grief, we experience nostalgia for that which is left behind, or homesickness, or a wistful longing for the good old days.

Aging therefore is the experience of passing a number of milestones and of celebrating the gains and the triumphs that have come our way. We need to celebrate birthdays, births, promotions, raises, anniversaries, and honors, to lift these good things up in our awareness, even while creating rites of passage. But aging can also be seen as the experience of sustaining a series of losses and of coping with the grief that is the appropriate and expectable feeling response to loss.

The writer to the Hebrews was right. Life is a journey or a quest. In the course of that journey we may cross long level places where the going is smooth; we may camp in pleasant places for a time. But we may have to cross burning desert wastes where water has to be rationed and the path is not clear. We may encounter steep hills to climb and roaring rivers to cross. Changes are transition points. Transitions put us to the test.

The Transitions of Later Maturity

A s we grow older, not all of us will face the same transitions or face them at the same age or deal with them in the same way. Not all of the transitions will be equally difficult or equally difficult for each person. Let's enumerate some of the common types of transitions that we could face in later maturity.

1. Those of us who are parents may have to discover new ways to use time, new ways to relate to husband or wife, and new outlets for concern and affection after children grow up and leave home. Although having children leave the nest is cause for some grief, many parents welcome it and find it both liberating and exhilarating. At any rate it marks a turning point in the pattern of living. It may pose the challenge of finding new ways of being a generative person rather than settling down and stagnating.

2. Those of us who are parents may have to work out new relationships with our children when they are grown and independent. Along with that we may have to learn how to be helpful grandparents. For so many years we have made decisions for our children, especially when they were small, that it may be hard to relinquish that role and let them live their own lives. They have been dependent on us for so long that it may be hard to let ourselves become dependent on them without being demanding or clinging. Interdependence and reciprocal relationships have to be worked at.

3. Many of us will need to find new ways of structuring our time, new outlets for our energies, new opportunities for association with others, and new social roles after retirement from an occupation. So much of identity is rooted in our work that we may face an identity crisis when we no longer work.

4. We may have to learn to be single again, perhaps to live alone again for a while, or to consider new forms of congregate

living arrangements. More than half of all women are widowed by the time they reach age 65. Forty-one percent of all older women live alone, and 15% of older men (6 million women, 1.7 million men). An additional 2% of both men and women live with nonrelatives. This raises questions about meeting and dating members of the opposite sex and of finding opportunities for relationships of intimacy and affection in which we may find confirmation of our own worth.

5. Many of us will find it convenient, appealing, or even necessary to move to a new community where we will be living in a new house. We will lose many familiar relationships and connections. We will need to establish an entirely new set of relationships: new doctor and dentist, new service persons, new insurance agents, new stores, and so on.

6. Some of us will have to come to terms with physical limitations we did not have in our earlier years. Some of us will have to get along with diminished sensory capacity.

Although none of these transitions are unique to later maturity, they are much more common in later maturity than in the younger years, which have their own characteristic common transitions.

Because so much of change is accompanied by pain and grief, we all tend to be conservatives. We try to keep our environment as stable as possible. We try to guard against the unexpected. But to live is to undergo change, and to love is to make a compact with sorrow. We need to reflect for a moment on the nature of grief and what is demanded as we do our grief work. Grieving usually is thought of only in relation to the bereavement through death of another person who is close to us. But there are many kinds of separation and losses that result in grief. To age successfully is to cope with the strain and the grief of making it through the transitions.

Patterns of grief work

The depth, duration, and pain of grief depend on the nature, extent, and meaning of the loss sustained. Grief is a complex and varied emotion. Each of us experiences it and expresses it in our own way. However, some or all of the following kinds of reactions may take place. To be aware of these reactions may help us to accept and to work through any grief we may experience.

First of all, we are likely to experience either shock or numbness or the inability to feel anything at all. We may have heart palpitations, loss of appetite, restlessness, and inability to concentrate, along with an inability to cry or show emotion. We may have a pervasive sense of emptiness.

This may be followed or accompanied by denial or disbelief: "Oh, no! This can't happen!" "There must be some mistake." Our denial may be extended by intake of drugs or alcohol or tranquilizers. It may be carried over into plunging into frenetic activity, as though nothing had happened. Sometimes even travel can be a way of denying the emptiness and the grief.

Shock and disbelief may be followed by an overwhelming sense of sorrow or outrage expressed in crying, moaning, or beating one's breast. This may be an important step in coming to terms with the loss, for it involves acceptance and outward expression of the feelings about loss. This may alternate with anger: "Why didn't they . . .?" Closely allied to anger is guilt. "If only I . . ." "Why didn't we . . .?" "I should have . . . before it was too late."

Eventually there comes a period of reorganization, when thought can be turned to the future, problems addressed, and plans laid. This will be a time when life comes back on a more or less even keel and we may even learn to laugh and to love again. As a friend and colleague of mine once put it, "I have decided to live again."

In the early stages of grief persons are likely to relive over and over again the events immediately associated with the loss itself. This is a part of the process of accepting the fact of the loss. This is followed by a tendency to go back over the past and the part that whatever is lost has played in it. The wife whose husband has died will recall the details of their life together, particularly the good things that happened and the meaning of the relationship. The man who has lost a leg may remember how he loved to run or play basketball. After that the bereaved person may begin to look ahead and plan for the future.

The classical picture of grief is that of the sorrow and remorse that follow a sudden, catastrophic bereavement, such as death following a short illness, a heart attack, or an auto accident. However, grief may come in anticipation of an impending loss or separation. The worker who knows that the plant is to be closed or that retirement is near may lose interest in the work and begin to distance himself psychologically from it. He may begin the process of transferring interests elsewhere. The discovery of a chronic degenerative disease such as Alzheimer's disease, or the realization a spouse is having a series of small strokes, or the diagnosis of terminal cancer sets up the grieving process. By the time of actual separation, much of the grief work may have been done. Sometimes a separation comes on gradually. A worker becomes aware of increasing disillusionment and dissatisfaction with a job. Marital partners and lovers may drift apart, communicating less and less on an intimate level. Gradually friends may lose touch with each other until they no longer even exchange Christmas cards. But anticipatory grief is real and can be painful.

Some grief may follow a "near-miss" situation on the part of a survivor of an epidemic or accident in which others have died, even though the survivor may not have been close to the ones who died. Some grief may follow recovery from a nearly fatal illness, as in the case of successful open-heart surgery in which life has been given back to one again. The separation here may be from a formerly rather thoughtless and carefree existence to the asking of such questions as: "Why was I spared?" "What must I do to pay for this?"

Coping with grief

The important thing in grief work is to face and accept the reality and finality of the loss—and with it the pain. Denial and repression may be important to allow one to catch one's breath, so to speak, but if prolonged it may leave a load of unfinished business and chronic depression. Repressed anger and unforgiven guilt have the same effect. Those who want to be helpful cannot force a person to accept loss. They can refrain from telling the grieving persons that they should not feel loss, that they should have a joyous faith, and there is nothing to be guilty about. Instead, they can stand by to share in the loss and the grief.

It is important to express what is felt, whether it be sorrow, anger, or guilt. These may be expressed through crying, through talking it out with a confidante, and through physical activity. In the movie *I Remember Mama,* Mama, a woman of few words, scrubbed the floors to work out her sorrow.

The emotions generated by the loss may release energy that can be converted to constructive purposes beyond the reconstruction of one's own life. Maggie Kuhn converted her anger over mandatory retirement and discrimination against women in pensions systems into the Grey Panther movement for reform. Women whose children were killed by drunken drivers— agitated for stricter laws against and stronger penalties for drunk drivers. Others, motivated by the compassion learned in their own sorrow, have turned to support others who have experienced a loss similar to theirs, whether of heart surgery, sight or hearing loss, mastectomy, or coping with Parkinson's and Alzheimer's diseases.

The final step toward the completion of grief work, of course, is to look for new centers of meaning, new affectional and intimate relationships to replace those that have been lost, new ways to structure time.

The memories, with the joy and the celebration of the meaning once held by that which has been lost, will always be there. The pain of loss will be there too. But if we have been successful in finding new outlets for energy, new sources of support, and new ways of investing time and energy, these losses may function as a reservoir from which we can draw understanding, compassion, and perspective.

Making it over the hump

One July day in California I stood on Mount Diablo watching my ten-year-old grandson practicing rock climbing under the tutelage of his father. He started to make his way up the face of a perpendicular sandstone cliff about 30 feet high. He used a diagonal crack in the face of the cliff for handholds and braced his toes against rough places on the rock as climbers do. He got along well until he came to a point about 15 feet up where the crack widened out and became an overhanging ledge. At that point the only way to go further up was to swing one knee up over the edge of the shelf while clinging to the edge with his fingers. This move required both strength in his arms and agility. It also involved a degree of risk, for he had to remove his feet from their position on the wall and grope blindly for a new handhold up and beyond the ledge.

In that instant the boy was overwhelmed by fear. He froze

to the side of the cliff, unable to go further. There was no easy way down. He buried his face in the crack to conceal his terror and his tears. Then he admitted defeat.

"I can't do it," he called down to his father. "I'm stuck. Help me down." His voice quivered with anxiety.

No amount of encouragement or instruction could nerve him to try to go on up. So we helped him down, standing below to catch him if he should slip and fall. When he was safely on the ground, his father went up the rock, showing him how it could be done.

About 15 minutes later, without a word to anyone or without any urging, my grandson was on the rock, climbing once more. He got to the place where he had been blocked before. Once again he faced the terror of swinging out and over the ledge. Again he froze. Again tears came to his eyes as shame mingled with the fear. He leaned into the rock to hide his terror. Then he summoned his courage and took the risk. He swung his foot up, caught the edge of the shelf with his knee, found a new handhold above. He wormed his body over the edge. With a shout of relief and triumph he was on his way up. "I did it!" he called down. "I did it!"

We face the loss of things we had counted on to make our journey successful, endurable, pleasant, and rewarding. We face the unknown, the risk of getting to a new plateau, and the call for the outpouring of additional energy. If the transition is small, we may have to make minor adjustments. If the transition is a major one, we may have to reorganize our whole lives.

After her husband died following a long, complicated, painful illness, after months of waiting, wondering, and hoping, a friend of mine said, "It's strange. I feel a great sense of relief, but at the same time suddenly a complete emptiness." She was only starting on her way through the transition. After the shock, the anger, and the bewilderment would come the need to find new patterns of daily existence and new structures of meaning. She would find it necessary to make all kinds of decisions and to struggle through compilations of financial arrangements, tax returns, and legal documents.

Living through transitions calls for courage. Courage is not the absence of fear or dread. Courage is the capacity to turn the adrenalin released by fear into action to transcend the danger. It is rooted in an inner strength that flows out of the deep sources of vitality or the will to live. Courage is found in the commitment to and support of others.

I know a successful, highly paid executive whose work had been his life. In line with company policy he was retired at age 65. Like so many of us, he had not allowed himself to accept the fact that it would happen to him and had not really faced what it would mean. Within a few days he lost the use of a company car with a driver, a reserved parking space, a secretary to receive his dictation and place his calls, and a generous expense account. Worst of all, he lost his status and the power it gave to make and effectuate decisions. He lost much that anchored his identity and his sense of worth as a person. He too came to a dead end. He too faced the terror and experienced the grief. At that time he had to summon up tremendous energy and begin to make a new life in a new community and to develop a new set of meaningful relationships and activities.

Living through transitions calls for faith: faith in ourselves and our capacity to change, faith in the worthwhileness of the journey, and faith in the mentors or guides we choose to follow through the transitions. Faith is an openness to the future and readiness to trust ourselves to uncertainty. By faith Abraham left Haran and went out, not knowing where he was going. Faith grows out of the experience of having discovered that there are things and persons we can rely on. It begins by taking risks and by testing ourselves against the challenge to change.

Angelina's mother reported that after she had learned to crawl, Angelina would pull herself up by the side of the playpen and stand there clinging to the bar and teetering. She did not know how to get back down, and she did not dare to let go for she feared the fall. So she cried until her mother came to help her down. But the day came when Angelina learned to let go and to sit down by herself, and then to let go and stand for a minute, and finally while standing to take some steps. Eventually she acquired the faith to walk and then to run, taking more tumbles along the way.

Faith also grows out of the learned expectation that life moves from one stage to another. It is rooted in the insight that we are sojourners and have here no continuing city. This gives us hope.

When our granddaughter was three years old, she found her "security blanket" in bits of colored ribbon that she carried at all times. One day when her grandmother announced she was going to the store, the little girl piped up to say she needed "a wibbon."

Her five-year-old brother was scornful, "I don't need a ribbon," he said, "and you don't need a ribbon."

The little girl retorted, "You are five years old. You don't need a wibbon. I am fwee years old. I need a wibbon." Then she added as an afterthought, "When I am five years old, I will not need a wibbon. Now I need a wibbon."

This must have started a chain of reflection, for she went on to say, almost to herself, "Now I suck my fumb. When I am five years old, I will not suck my fumb." In a moment this was followed by the triumphant announcement, "And when I am five years old, I will wake up dwy every morning."

As every hiker or climber knows, the hiking or climbing itself is enjoyable—as well as the destination. We test our resources, we discover our strengths, we thrill to the changing views we see along the way. At the same time we sustain the bumps, we face the terror occasionally, we withstand some pain while we confirm our capacity to endure and to overcome, drawn onward by the hope of the glory to be experienced when we arrive. Once we arrive, we begin to think about the next trip.

What we need to remember is that a major loss or traumatic bereavement may be the doorway to a new life if we can surmount the pain and the grief. The pain and the grief are real, but they can be transcended through faith and the work of making the transition.

Faith is sustained, courage is released, and hope is nourished by the knowledge that others have gone on before us and have made the transitions and have experienced the glory of achievement on the other side. So it is that the writer of the letter to the Hebrews reminds us to look to Jesus, whom he calls the "author and perfecter of our faith, who for the joy set before him endured the cross, scorning its shame, and sat down at the right hand of the throne of God" (Heb. 12:2).

The cross stands as a symbol for the destruction of that which we hold most dear and at the same time for the doorway to a new and better life. Without the crucifixion there would be no resurrection. Living is something like going up a ladder. We have to let go of one rung in order to get up to the next. It is important to have a sturdy ladder well planted on a solid base, but there is no way to go up except by risking one step after another.

By accepting change as a given, and by recognizing that every once in a while we face a transition, we can learn to move on, even though painfully, and to reorganize our lives on a higher level.

One day I sat at the dinner table with a 94-year-old gentleman who had lost almost all of his eyesight. I admired the adeptness with which he managed his eating. I complimented him on how well he did.

"Thank you," he said. "But you know you can learn almost anything if you have to." Then his face lighted up and he said, "I like to learn. I have lots of curiosity. I can hardly wait to see what is going to happen next."

The writer to the Hebrews calls the roll of the heroes of the faith, beginning with Abel and leading up to Jesus. He describes what they went through as they moved out in faith, pursuing their quest. Then he notes that none of them actually received what was promised for, "God had planned something better for us so that only together with us would they be made perfect" (Heb. 11:40).

Some years ago a movie was made of the life of Madame Marie Curie, who discovered that radium was the source of the X ray. She came as a young chemistry student to Paris, where she met her husband Pierre. Together they became fascinated by this X ray that left its traces on photographic film. So they set out to see if they could find and isolate the element responsible. They could get no support for their project. They toiled in poverty. Ill from the cold and malnourishment, Pierre tried to dissuade Marie from the quest. The price seemed too high. But she would not be turned aside. In the movie she says, "I do not know if I will be able to find it or not. But some day someone will. I have to see how far I can get in my lifetime."

A favorite anthem of mine is titled "The Journey Is My Home." Since we have here no continuing city, we move out in faith, seeking a city with foundations, whose builder and maker is God. As we do so, we elect to face the terror of the unknown. We take the risk of falling. We endure the pain for the hope of the glory on the other side, knowing that we cannot go back. We go forward, knowing that we are not the first who has gone this way and that we are not alone. We are a part of a long line of pioneers, carrying out our part of the mission assigned to the human race, until all of us make it to the mountaintop, and our journey here is ended, and we make the transition to that which lies beyond.

CHAPTER THREE

Saying Amen to All of Life

The opening chapters of the book of Genesis tell how God created the world. According to the story there, when it was all done, God stepped back and surveyed his handiwork. "And God saw everything that he had made, and behold, it was very good" (Gen. 1:31). That affirmation appears again and again in the Bible: "It was very good." It is a basic implication of the historic creeds.

But then we contemplate the prospect of getting old, and when we see the wasted wrecks of bodies and ruined minds of so many in their last years, and when we remember how persons we have known and loved faded away in the twilight of their lives, it becomes difficult for us to join in that ascription of praise to the Creator for his creation. True, most of us are grateful to be alive. Most of us cherish the thought of living a long time. But as we assess the probabilities that accident and disease will subject us to pain and disability in our old age, we find it hard to say "Amen!" to all of that. Even if we do manage to escape the surgeon's knife or the wheelchair, eventually our powers will wane and our dependence will increase. Who can celebrate that?

Surely, if creation was originally good, something must have gotten fouled up along the line so that creation is now hopelessly marred with the taint of evil. When Adam and Eve pushed beyond the limits of Eden, their eyes were opened, they became conscious of the difference between good and evil, they lost their paradise, and they learned that life was hard. Birth was risky and painful. Survival demanded great effort. Disease and accident plagued them on every side. (The fossil bones of earliest human beings evidence arthritis.) Predators dogged their steps, waiting to pounce and devour. Before long their own children turned on each other, and Cain murdered Abel. Blood, sweat, and tears are the price we pay for our brief existence here.

Sometimes the affirmations of religious faith seem absurd in the face of human experience. It may be that, among all the other troubles we endure, the vicissitudes of aging, more than anything else, cause us to hesitate before affirming that creation is good.

In spite of the optimistic dreams of some that aging might be avoided and death postponed indefinitely by the magic of technology, aging still is inevitable and inescapable, invariably culminating in our death.

Death, to the apostle Paul, was the last enemy to be destroyed by God, having come into being through sin (1 Cor. 15:26; Rom. 5:12-14).

Many modern writers and poets have expressed some of the same sentiment. While 19th-century figures such as Robert Browning and Alfred Lord Tennyson had a positive view of aging, others who came later, such as William Butler Yeats and Dylan Thomas for example, did not.

William Butler Yeats, who died in 1939 at the age of 74, railed against becoming older. He feared that he would lose his lyric gift as he grew older since he relied on his anger and his lust to fuel his poetic impulse. He wondered if everyone raged as he did against old age, believing that only young men could dream. However, he finally made peace with the burden of his years and was able to affirm what he called a "tragic joy" as he began to face the mystery of approaching death. Indeed, he kept on writing until a few weeks before his death.

Dylan Thomas, too, expressed this universal feeling when he wrote out of the grief over the death of his father. He shouted out that one should not take death calmly or die gently. One should be angry that it had to happen and rage against it, fighting all the way. We do not know what he might have felt if he had not died while still young.

W. Andrew Achenbaum, in his history of the American experience with aging (*Old Age in a New Land,* Johns Hopkins, 1978) maintains that while Americans have always recognized the losses of old age, it was only after the Civil War that Americans began to think of the elderly as roleless, unproductive, and disengaged from life. They were regarded as those who could teach how to live a long and productive life, they served as guardians of virtue, they made significant contributions in many capacities in their communities. The industrial revolution, the rise of technology and specialized scientific knowledge, and the development of bureaucracy engendered disesteem for the elderly and the veneration of youth.

Ronald Blythe's study of old age in Great Britain entitled *The View in Winter: Reflections on Old Age* tends to give a bleak outlook on the later years.[1] Robert Butler's study of *Why Survive? Being Old in America,* intended to call attention to the need for better social policies, services, and institutions to care for dependent older people, reinforces the bleak perspective on senescence.[2]

My mother lived to be almost 90. She was a pioneer woman, homesteading first with her parents and then with my father in the sandhills of Nebraska. My father, who was 13 years older than she, died when she was 54, a year after he retired from ranching. Shortly thereafter her youngest child contracted poliomyelitis and had to be nursed through long months of a nearly fatal and finally crippling illness. To earn a living my mother then bought and operated a country store in Iowa. At the age of 58 she married a widower; together they moved to Minnesota to buy and operate a farm. When she was around 70, they sold their livestock, rented out the farmland and barns, and retired, limiting themselves to growing flowers and a vegetable garden.

When she was 78 her second husband died after a year of increasing frailty. Up to that time she had never lived alone and had always had someone who needed her. Life began to close in on her from that time on. After a year of living in rotation with her children, she settled in a small apartment near one of her daughters. Finally even that became too much to care for. Living with her children was not a satisfactory solution. She moved into a retirement hotel. The last four years of her life she began to fail noticeably. Her eyesight gradually grew dim, so she had to give up the needlework she had enjoyed all her life. Her hearing diminished to the point that going to church or enjoying large gatherings became difficult. She could neither read nor enjoy watching television. Then two years before her death a hip broke, requiring surgery and a stay in a convalescent hospital. This was the first time in her life she had had a broken bone, had required surgery, or had been in a hospital (her six babies had all been born at home). She was bewildered and frightened, scared and ashamed at the need to be completely dependent on strangers. Out of the hospital and ambulatory again, she began to lose control of her bowel and bladder movements. She had occasional accidents, which she tried to ignore or treat as a joke because of her embarrassment. After that she began to forget things. Another broken hip put her in a nursing home. The last six months of her life she was completely incontinent and unable to recognize or respond to anyone.

My wife's mother had a series of strokes that finally left her partially paralyzed and in need of continual nursing care. The last few months of her life she lived with us, confined to her room most of the time. She died suddenly of a massive cerebral hemorrhage as I was sitting beside her bed reading to her.

Isaac Bashevis Singer, in an author's note to *The Penitent,* recalled saying in an interview that

> I voiced a severe protest against creation and the Creator
> . . . .although I believed in God and admired His divine wisdom, I could not see or glorify his mercy. . . .if I were able to picket the Almighty, I would carry a sign with the slogan UNFAIR TO LIFE.[3]

The Ills of Old Age

Many of our fears of old age are rooted in an inaccurate image of old age. The probability that we will experience debilitating sickness, poverty, loneliness, dementia, and uselessness is much smaller than popularly believed. Nevertheless, many of us will experience one or more of these ills. Just as there are debits that detract from the unlimited enjoyment of youth, or young adulthood, or middle age, so there are things that rather commonly fret most of us in later maturity. These are real.

To begin with, there is the realization that time is running out for us and that many of our fondest hopes and most cherished dreams have been unrealized, while the list of failures, disappointments, losses, and frustrations have piled up. In our later years we may have to give up the drive for high office, the acquisition of power, the amassing of wealth, the hope of becoming famous. We may have to accept the fact that we have left no line of progeny to carry on the family name or that the children in whom we invested such hope are after all just ordinary and occasionally disappointing.

Closely associated with time running out is the loss of status and a significant and respected role in the community, either because of our age and the depreciation of age in the culture or because of retirement and the loss of power. As long as we hold an office in which we can influence or enforce decisions, as long as we have wealth to distribute or to withhold, or as long as we have technical skills and proven knowledge that are in demand, we command respect. Otherwise respect has to be grounded in gratitude for past achievement, admiration of what we have been able to become, or affection because of what we are.

Another debit against later maturity is the loss of sexual and physical attractiveness, related to the disgust and devaluation of aging bodies endemic in our society and to the waning sexual drive or potency. These threaten our confidence in our ability to attract friends, particularly of the opposite sex, and to receive affection. Most people enjoy touching the skin of a baby but are repelled by the wrinkles of old age. Because sex, intimacy, and the confirmation of worth are so closely tied together, later years make it more difficult to be close to a circle of confidants.

Also, there tends to be an increase in the number and frequency of aches and pains associated with the wear and tear suffered over the years. This often comes along with the annoyance or inconvenience caused by eyes that are not as sharp or hearing that is not as acute or taste that is not as keen.

So, having made the worst case against later maturity, we raise again the question of how we can affirm the goodness of creation and say "Amen!" to all of life. Why would God create a world in which all things from rocks to human flesh grow old and die?

Aging carries us through many changes. Many of them can be celebrated as gains. Knowledge can increase, as can serenity, perspective, wisdom, and satisfaction in achievement. We can rejoice in the accumulated years to the extent that they are replete with happy memories and have enlarged the circle of those who love us and whom we have loved. But many changes bring losses to be mourned. Many of them are attended by pain. Some of us die full of years. Some of us are cut off too soon. Some die quickly and quietly. Some slide into conditions of disability and even of coma that may go on for months, even years.

Think now. If you had been the Creator, what kind of a world would you have made? Would you have designed a world in which creatures grow old and die? Would you have made a world in which there is constant change? As one of my friends, a beautiful woman who has Parkinson's disease, said, "I will tolerate my disease, but I will never accept it!"

We can look at the data presented by life and draw different conclusions, depending on which set of filters we use in screening and sorting the data, or which set of glasses we use to view them. If we are bent toward pessimism, we can find support for our expectation of misery. If we are inclined toward optimism, we can find justification for the conclusion that the loving, creating, reconciling, satisfying aspects of life far outweigh the negative. Suffering can be magnified, or it can be put in the perspective of a short path to an eternal crown of glory and of bliss, as did the apostle Paul (2 Cor. 4:16-18).

Mr. Thomas was once a charming, intelligent, successful man. In his 70s he lost both his sight and his hearing, in spite of all the specialists could do. He then withdrew into himself and indicated he wanted to die. He refused to eat. He resisted the efforts of others to communicate with him. He sank into a state of chronic anger and frustration, relieved only by sedation. He had to be restrained, otherwise he would injure himself by slamming his head against the wall.

Mrs. Rolafson lost her power of speech and ability to walk because of a progressive nervous disease. However, she coped valiantly. She learned to spell out words by pointing with a stick to letters on an alphabet board. She eagerly reached out to others. All along, her disposition was sunny.

The apostle Paul had experienced the nagging pain of a thorn in the flesh. He had been beaten by mobs, rejected by most of his fellow countrymen, jailed by the authorities on trumped-up charges. He had been shipwrecked, stranded on a primitive island, and had gone without food. Yet while he and Silas lay chained in a dungeon, imprisoned on false charges, at midnight they sang hymns of praise to God. How was he able to take a joyous, hopeful view of life, affirming the goodness of creation in the bleakest of circumstances?

Roots of Paul's Optimism

1. We are loved

To begin with, Paul *had become aware that he was loved unconditionally.* He had experienced complete acceptance from others in spite of actions which could have caused him to be rejected. He was cared for by those whom he had persecuted. He not only experienced being loved, but he saw love being manifested around him to others. He watched as Stephen died praying for those who were stoning him to death.

Paul had been touched and transformed by an encounter with the living Christ, the Spirit of love and creativity embodied in a human group, the disciples of Christ. This encounter shattered most of his previously held ideas. It reversed his attitude toward the followers of the Way. It fused a reintegration of his personality. When he was linked up to a community of persons who cared about him, he was made aware that he was linked up with a God who cared about him and that God's love was unconditional. God's love was given freely, not because Paul had earned it nor because Paul had been able to live a completely righteous life, but because God valued Paul for himself alone.

So it was that Paul could write:

> For I am convinced that neither death, nor life, nor angels nor demons, neither the present nor the future, nor any powers, neither height nor depth, nor anything else in all creation, will be able to separate us from the love of God that is in Christ Jesus our Lord (Rom. 8:38-39).

Paul had thought that he would not be loved unless he perfectly fulfilled the letter of the law. He carried a burden of guilt over the sins he had been unable to avoid. He thought his value depended on his success. He was obsessed with his own shortcomings and those of others. In fighting against them he was drawn more deeply into the quagmire of guilt and rage. Then he discovered that he was loved in spite of his imperfections and his unacceptableness and his failures. He was forgiven freely without having to make reparations. He could rest in God's grace rather than depend on his own efforts. He was set free to focus his life on loving others rather than on the eradication of sin and heresy.

God's strategy of salvation is that of the incarnation, the expression of the divine love through human relationships. Those who have discovered that they have been and are loved are much more likely to say "Amen!" to life. So Paul came to see love as the dominant factor in the world, active in overcoming the negative, hostile, destructive forces rampant all around. God had sent his Son into the world because he loved the world. Love was overcoming the world. So Paul aligned himself with the forces of love and celebrated that love.

2. We are made in God's image

In the second place, Paul *discovered that he was given the possibility of being a cocreator, a partner with God, in the making and redeeming of the world.* He came to believe that by working with the central creative force that was moving upon the face of chaos, he could make a difference in what the world would become. Also, he came to believe that this world would at last be perfected in glory, a glory in which we could share. So he found both possibility and purpose.

Reporting on interviews with 623 persons, Lisle Marburg Goodman concluded that

> The more complete one's life is, the more one's destiny and one's creative capacities are fulfilled, the less one fears death. . . . People are not afraid of death per se, but of the incompleteness of their lives.[4]

Persons need to be involved in life projects that have significance.

In his 70s Paul Tournier wrote in *Learn to Grow Old:*

> I cannot repeat what I hear so often, and what is expected of me, that the meaning of my old age is to prepare me for death and for meeting God, to detach me from the things of the world in order to attach me to those of heaven. . . . Death is not a project, and it is not my reality. *What concerns me is my life now, and to seek the will of God for me today. . . . My life as it is today has a meaning.*[5]

Rubem Alves, the Brazilian theologian, says that for the Christian "the primary fact is not that of death but rather of life." He goes on to say that when one is made free for life, one is able to run the risk of dying for the sake of contributing to a new world. In his words, "Authentic life cannot be separated from the subjective possibility of transforming the earth."[6]

Persons can affirm the goodness of creation if they have found that within certain limits they can create the world in which they live. They need to know that their efforts do make a difference in the way things are, and that these differences will have a lasting effect.

I am quite aware that social and cultural pressures can warp personality, particularly in the early years of life when the person is most vulnerable. I know that an impoverished environment can have a constricting effect on what one is able to do, because it reduces opportunities. I understand that destructive attitudes and cultural patterns can be passed on from one generation to another by means of the socialization process. But I cannot accept the idea that we are only passive respondents or victims without possibility of choice. We can assume responsibility for changing our world. We can exercise creativity in coping with the problems we face. We can decide within limits what kinds of persons we are going to be.

Persons are bound and caught in the toils of sin, not only because we are sinful beings but also because sin becomes institutionalized in social structures. But grace, too, is operative within us and within the world we inhabit. There are structures of grace within the human community through which the Holy Spirit moves. No persons have been left without some witness to the power and love of God, if we can but see it. The gospel is that we are empowered and set free to make a difference, that we do not need to accept our lot supinely and passively, that we can realize some of our potential. But we have to decide to accept the gift, to allow grace to have sway.

Robert Coles, a Harvard psychiatrist, has been studying the effects of poverty and the meaning of the civil rights movement among minority groups, especially among children. He spent some time in the Southwest trying to discover what growing up meant among Americans of Hispanic background.[7] He was directed by them to talk with the grandparents, because it was they who were regarded as having the most influence on the lives of children. As he talked with these older people, he discovered that although they had led lives of poverty and had suffered both oppression and the contempt of the dominant Anglo group, they had preserved their dignity. They maintained a firm belief that they were persons to be valued and respected. Their survival and safety needs had barely been met. The wider society had demeaned and often rejected them. But they displayed toughness and persistence in coping with adversity. They had a consciousness of personal integrity. They had found a sense of belonging, and they had received affection. Within the family, among their peers, and in their church they found a transcendent meaning for their lives.

3. We die to rise again

In the third place, Paul *came to see that dying was the passage to a new life.* One had to let go of that which *is* for the sake of that which *is to be.* Loving means being willing to let go. The bird in the hand dies from suffocation. The bird released soars into the sky, where it is free to sing. Life is a series of renunciations of some alternatives in order to make the commitments that enable life to go on. We have here no continuing city. God's creation involves a series of transformations, transmutations, and separations. To be born is to be ejected from the security of the womb. To grow up is to take responsibility for one's self and to leave the safety of the parental nest. To take advantage of new opportunities to serve, to create, or to further one's career is to separate oneself from the routines that may have been comfortable.

Dying is experienced every time we face a major change or suffer a significant loss. Consider the lifelong relation of a parent to a child. My daughter is born, and I become deeply attached to her. She grows from a babbling baby into a delightful little girl. I take her to kindergarten and leave her in the hands of a stranger for the day. The little girl becomes a big girl and then a young woman. She graduates from high school. She goes off to college in a distant city, and we see her only occasionally during the year. She graduates from college and finishes her preparation for a career, becoming economically self-sufficient. The day comes when I give her in marriage to a handsome young man. Then she leaves her first home altogether to establish a home of her own.

At each stage I die a little and grieve at the loss of that which has been. Each transition is marked by sadness or nostalgia, even though at the same time I rejoice to see the child mature into an autonomous adult who relates to me as an equal. It is not always easy to make these renunciations. Even when the renunciations are made, all that has been is still a part of me. So it is with each person I love.

Paul had learned how to die by experiencing many losses, by giving up outmoded but cherished convictions and commitments, and by discovering that in the surrender of the past the future opens to new possibilities. In his early manhood he saw his life as a fortress to be guarded against the forces that would change it; he lived with a siege mentality. After his conversion he became a pilgrim on the open road, following a moving star. Paul was able to endure the toils of aging and to face the prospect of death because of an unshakable conviction in the resurrection of Christ and the assurance of his resurrection in Christ.

Paul had learned that beyond every death there is the possibility of resurrection to a new life on a new level. He was confirmed in this faith by the awareness that Jesus of Nazareth continued to live as the Christ within and among those who called themselves by his name. All who have lost persons dear to them, who have lived through the failure of hopes and projects, who have known the heartbreak of fire, flood, famine, or war, and who have survived to experience new love, new projects, and new purpose understand what it means to die and to rise again into a new life.

4. We have assurance of life eternal

Finally, Paul *saw his life as being set within the context of the whole history of the human race and even beyond that within the context of the creation and fulfillment of the whole universe.* He saw himself as the connecting link between generations, a part of the chain of life. He draws on this insight in Romans 8 when he talks about the whole creation being in travail, waiting for its perfecting.

No one is complete in himself, but within the life process each individual person has an important role to play. At any time humankind is only one generation away from the loss of civilization. Our failure to conserve and to enhance what has been given to us deprives all subsequent generations. In *Wind, Sand, and Stars* Antoine de Saint-Exupery suggests that each person ought to think of himself as a sentry stationed at some lonely outpost of empire.[8] Rather than bemoaning the fact that we have such a minor part to play in such an insignificant corner of the world, we ought to remember that the safety and security of all the rest of the human race depend on our faithfulness to our duty. It could be that if we were to go to sleep or desert our posts or flee without a struggle when a threat comes, the empire could be overcome through that single gap in the line.

Standing sentry in the cold and windy night, alone and exposed, is no easy task and is not without hardship, but it is a significant task. So, too, our lives have significance in the struggle of a world being created. Our death and the deaths of others we care for are but episodes in this timeless drama.

Let the Congregation Say Amen!

As we come to understand why the Apostle Paul could say "Amen!" to all of life, we can find reasons why we too can affirm the basic goodness of creation in spite of pain, suffering, and human tragedy. We can find clues for taking a positive attitude in our approach to later maturity. This by itself can become a self-fulfilling prophecy, for life will become in many ways what we expect and will be what we focus on and perceive.

1. Count your blessings

First of all, while aware of the tragic background of existence we can *stop harping on the bad things* that have happened to us and *balance the account by counting the good things* that we have been privileged to experience. This is not to deny, like Pollyanna, the real pain we feel, but to focus on the loving and the creating forces permeating existence.

The worship of the early church primarily was thanksgiving. It centered in the Eucharist in recognition of the fact that God already had acted and salvation had been accomplished. So often as I attend services of worship, the note that predominates is that of "concerns," pleas for help and healing, and intercession for the sick. I seldom hear thanksgiving for those who have recovered. We seem to forget that we have already been rescued, forgiven, brought into newness of life. In the Psalms, even those which plead with God to help the petitioner out of trouble, the one who prays begins by remembering what God has already done in the past.

Some persons seem to be injustice collectors, not only overly sensitive but actually on the lookout for dirty deals. To them every silver lining must have its cloud. Their suspiciousness and defensiveness often precipitate the very thing they are expecting. Bitterness and resentment generate the kind of reactions from others that feed the anger.

But while some persons collect insults, others gather butterflies. They are especially sensitive to moments of beauty and acts of kindness. Their trust stimulates responsibility in others. They do not expect perfection. They are ready to forgive, because they appreciate the pressure others are under and the hurts others have received. They seek to understand rather than to condemn. Because they are more relaxed and less anxious, they actually may experience less pain.

When eyesight and hearing dim and persons become forgetful, they receive ambiguous signals and poorly defined clues about what is going on around them. So they tend to guess and to fill in the gaps by using their imaginations. All of us do that, even under the best of situations. Those who tend to be generally suspicious and distrustful are inclined to imagine the worst. Those who are basically trusting without being gullible imagine more positive things.

Let me suggest an exercise. Do it now or during your period of meditation. Take a sheet of graph paper or a plain piece of paper. Draw a line in the middle to divide the paper the long way. Mark this horizontal axis line off into five- or ten-year intervals from zero to 100. Put a dot on the line to mark the age where you are now. The figure below illustrates how this will look.

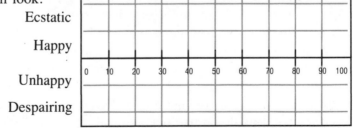

The vertical axis on this graph will represent life satisfaction. The space above the line represents happiness, that below the line unhappiness. For each five- or ten-year interval put a dot marking the high points and the low points. Connect the dots so you have a continuous line. Are there more highs or more lows? Which period of your life was the best? If you could stop the clock, so to speak, and live the rest of your life in one period, which one would you choose?

Finally, complete the line for the rest of your life, estimating how many years you may have yet to live. Will it get better? worse? up and down?

As we get older, it is useful for us to engage in a review of our lives and to reflect on our experience to see what we can learn from it for the future and how we can put it all together. Of course, we must do this with compassion for our developing selves and for those who had an influence on us. We need to remember all those times when we have been loved or when we have been given gifts by others.

A long life is a gift. Old age is a gift which many of us would not have been able to enjoy a generation ago. Abraham Heschel has said, "To be is a blessing. To live is holy!"[9] So let us join the psalmist in singing,

Praise the Lord, O my soul;
all my inmost being, praise his holy name.
Praise the Lord, O my soul,
and forget not all his benefits (Ps. 103:1-2).

2. Light a candle

Next, we can exercise our option to *be cocreators with God of a better world,* setting ourselves to bring order and beauty out of the chaos around us. The response to being loved is to be loving. Love is creative.

We older people can refuse to accept a secondary status in society, can demand that we be accorded both respect and opportunity to participate in the production and the distribution of the world's goods—material and spiritual. We can begin to change the image of aging and the attitudes people have toward later maturity. We can take charge of our lives. We can assume responsibility for the way we relate to others. We can be an instrument for the working of the Holy Spirit.

The Shepherd's Center in Kansas City was founded on this principle by the Reverend Elbert Cole in 1972. Some 600 older adults, including retired professionals, are involved in volunteer service. As a part-time consultant and trainer I have been helping to organize similar centers across the nation. At the same time I am one of the volunteers in the original center. These persons have changed the way many people in Kansas City view aging and older adults.

We can make a long list of persons who have made a difference in their later years and who left the world a better place because of what they did in their later years. We note the names of Albert Schweitzer, Pablo Casals, Arturo Toscanini, Archibald MacLeish, and Grandma Moses. We note also the names of Lillian Martin, who founded the first counseling center for older people in San Francisco after her retirement in the 1930s; Wilma Donahue, who brought into being the Institute on Aging at the University of Michigan; Ethel Percy Andrus, who founded the American Association of Retired Persons; Ollie Randall, for her work in nurturing the National Council on Aging into being; and Maggie Kuhn, who sparked the Grey Panthers. All these used their last years to enrich life and to bring hope and beauty into the world.

Around the country many high-rise apartment houses are being built for the low-income disabled and elderly. They often bring together persons from many different backgrounds who do not know each other and have little in common other than their age or income level. Living alone in such an apartment house can be a grim and lonely experience.

As I accompanied a pastor on a visit to such an apartment house in an inner-city area, she remarked that these dwellings were much like concentration camps. Most of the residents were there because they had no other choice. They tended to be incarcerated because they did not know their neighbors and were too timid to make the effort. They were shut in by their fear of going out on the street where they might be mugged. They were imprisoned because they had no transportation and were baffled by the public transportation system.

In her book *Unexpected Community,* A. R. Hochschild tells how residents in one such apartment house began to form a new community and to establish a network of meaningful relationships that set them free.[10] They developed new communal activities, new cultural patterns, and new rites to deal with traumatic events. This was happening in the apartment house the pastor and I were visiting because she had succeeded in getting them to meet and get acquainted while waiting in line to get blood-pressure checks once a month. They got a dairy to drop off supplies of milk, which they then delivered. They formed a committee to plan a spaghetti supper once a month. They appointed monitors of each wing on each floor to check on the well-being of their neighbors. A weekly Bible-study class was organized. These older people were beginning to take charge of their own lives and to create a new world.

Even though a person is caught in a nursing home with much loss of power over her own life and with the dehumanization that takes place in relation to institutional routines, she can still have some effect on her world. Miss Saterlee, a retired school teacher, is confined to bed and wheelchair in a nursing home. But because of her affectionate and appreciative response to those who come her way, aides and nurses love her in return and, as much as time allows, treat her with tenderness. But Miss Conway, a retired bookkeeper in the same nursing home, because of her bitter attitude toward life and her obvious contempt for the nursing staff, can hardly expect the same treatment, and even if she does, she will not feel the same about it.

On his TV program *On the Road* Charles Kuralt showed the film of a man he met in Minnesota who, after retirement, took on the project of building a road when he was unable to persuade county or state officials to do it. For a decade he had been working at it with an old tractor, a wheelbarrow, and a shovel—all by himself. He has a purpose. He is creating a better world by leaving behind him a road over which others will be able to travel with greater ease.

3. Look for the open doors

Again, we can *accept change and loss as realities of a life and a world which is in process,* but which open new possibilities and new challenges. The Spirit of God may work through the closing of doors as well as the opening of doors.

Aging and dying of individuals are ways in which the species of living creatures are rejuvenated, improved, and developed. Try to picture a world in which nothing moves, nothing changes, nothing grows, and nothing dies. That would be a static world, a world of negativity, a world without a future. It would be a world sterile of interest, suspense, challenge, or adventure. It would be a world with nothing to strive for, nothing to look forward to. It would be a world without incentive toward the best use of time. Hell might be such a place, where boredom would be the worst of all problems.

In his 80s, Archibald MacLeish wrote a poem entitled "Calypso's Island" in which he reflects on change. He speaks through the voice of the Greek warrior Ulysses, who has been trying for years to get back home after the Trojan Wars. Ulysses has been cast upon an island ruled by the goddess Calypso who not only is very beautiful but also is immortal. She falls in love with Ulysses and tries to persuade him to stay with her by promising to make him immortal too. But Ulysses remembers his wife Penelope back home in Ithaca and tries to explain why he wants to return home. He acknowledges the beauty of Calypso and the mortality of Penelope who will grow older and die. But he tells Calypso that in spite of all that he still yearns to contend again with the ocean waves and to be back home where the seasons change and where the one he loves too must die.

New life can open after retirement with new freedom to be and to do, to make new friends, and to discover new areas of meaningful activity. Mrs. Angus, daughter of a sharecropper, was reared in poverty and deprivation, given only limited schooling. She was married three times. She worked hard all her life, rearing a family of sons and daughters in the ghetto of a northern city. But late in life, after her family was grown and she was able to retire, she extended her volunteer activities to become involved in the civil-rights struggle, seeking opportunity and aid for the people of her community. Eventually she was appointed to the mayor's and then the governor's committee on aging. For the first time in her life she attended national conferences, made speeches, and put on a long dress to sit down at banquets, loved and respected as "a mother in Israel."

4. Look at life in the context of eternity

Finally, we can *look at our individual lives as transcendent to time and earthly existence.* Saint Augustine was Bishop of Hippo in North Africa when the Roman Empire was at the point of collapse. Barbarian armies were sacking the cities as the empire was falling apart. It was then that he had a vision of the City of God as enduring beyond the cities of men. His vision became a force in enabling a new social order to come into being in Europe on the ruins of the old.

There is change all around us and within us. The universe itself is in turmoil and undergoing travail. In fact, the universe is said to be running down, and in time the earth itself will grow old and die, unable to support life as we know it. But new stars are being born. New galaxies may start to spin. I participate in that process of creation even though I grow old. Even better, my growing old is a part of my participation in that process. So I will continue to participate in the glory of God the Creator forever and ever.

Let the congregation say "Amen!" to all of life and all the years.

CHAPTER FOUR

Singing at Midnight

When our children were small, we bought a set of children's encyclopedias. Our five-year-old daughter was fascinated. One day she asked her mother to read to her the article on snakes, which was illustrated with beautiful colored pictures. The article pointed out that some of the snakes were poisonous and dangerous because their bite might cause death. When they had finished reading the article, the child asked, "Mommy, did God make snakes?"

"Why, yes," her mother answered. "God made all things. So he made snakes too."

"But," the child persisted, "did he mean to?"

A child voiced a question most of us ask at one time or another. In a simple way she phrased a problem over which all philosophies and all theologies stumble—the problem of evil.

Certainly evil exists, and we see evidences of suffering all around us.

A young man goes to a party and imbibes too freely of alcoholic beverages. He gets in his car to go home. He loses control of the car and slams head-on into another car.

A family of four on their way home from visiting relatives are killed; another person is maimed for life; one driver escapes with bruises.

Hoodlums break into the home of a couple, both of whom are in their 90s, and beat them badly. The woman is killed immediately, the man lingers on for a week in the hospital.

A man suffers excruciating pain from rheumatoid arthritis while slowly but inexorably becoming more and more disabled during the last 15 years of his life. A contemporary of his stays well and vigorous until he dies peacefully in his sleep at age 95.

A tornado suddenly forms and destroys an entire neighborhood.

We're left with the questions. Why this one? Why not that one? Why evil?

Evil is that which "thwarts continuously and severely the potential goodness of creation, destroying alike its intelligibility and meaning, and making life as we experience it so threatening and so full of sorrow, and apparently pointless," as Langdon Gilkey put it.[1] Evil is that which is contrary to the mind and spirit of Jesus Christ. It is that which violates love of God and love of neighbor. It is that which destroys the unity of life, of the community, and of the world.

In human life, and especially in old age, evil is experienced as physical pain from which there is no surcease and which seems to have no lifesaving value as a warning of danger. It is experienced as neglect, rejection, and humiliation. It is experienced as life empty of meaning and the future void of hope. It is experienced as the diminution of sensory capacities and progressive disablement of function. Evil is experienced as the erosion of self because of some mind-destroying disease.

It is hard to deal with the fact that evil exists. It is even harder to explain why suffering is so unequally distributed among us. It is still more difficult to live with the suffering when it is visited on us or on those close to us. That is one side of the coin.

The other side of the coin is that in spite of suffering, many persons have learned how to endure suffering gracefully, to rise above the pain, and to find joy in the midst of it.

If any person ever had occasion to rail against fate, it was the apostle Paul. Acts 16 describes how Paul and Silas tried to be helpful to a slave girl who was being exploited and abused by her owners. The owners retaliated by falsely accusing Paul and Silas of immorality and of disturbing the peace. The apostles were then brutalized by the mob. The authorities, who should have protected them, illegally threw them into prison. They were chained in the dungeons instead of being given an impartial trial. Most of us would have burned with anger, filled with apprehension if not despair. But when midnight came Paul and Silas were praying and singing hymns to God. As they sang, the prison doors were opened, their jailor was converted, and they were set free.

So we have here two key questions related to each other: First, why do we suffer, and particularly why is suffering so unequally distributed? Second, how can we cope with suffering and learn to sing at midnight? How can we live with tragedy without giving way to either cynicism or despair?

Explanations of Evil

Through the centuries many brilliant minds have struggled with the question of evil and suffering. Many answers have been given. We, too, cannot help but keep on asking with the psalmists, "Why?" and "How long?"

Evil as the misuse of freedom

One ancient and still common answer to the question of why people suffer is that the person who is afflicted is being punished for wrongdoing. At times this answer has some immediate plausibility. It is obvious that in some situations the pain has been brought on the sufferer's own actions—through greed, carelessness, lust, or stupidity—in which he or she has willfully or ignorantly violated the commonsense rules of hygiene, safety, or fair play. We value health, and we want the best of medical care when we are sick, but we stubbornly keep on doing those things that destroy our health or jeopardize our well-being. Then we complain about the high cost of being cured. The American Health Association has estimated that 50% of the deaths that occurred in 1982 were brought on by life-style decisions and could have been prevented.

Sometimes we know beforehand that things we are going to do will be harmful. But we do them anyway, even in spite of good resolutions. Or else we rationalize "It won't hurt this one time," or "It can't do any harm to me." Paul puzzled about this when he wrote, "What I want to do I do not do, but what I hate I do" (Rom. 7:15).

Furthermore, there is enough free-floating guilt in most of us, enough of the feeling that we deserve to be punished, that we too often accept what happens to us or those close to us as retribution for our sin. When my wife and I learned that our three-year-old son was deaf, we kept asking ourselves, as parents of children with handicapping conditions usually do, "What did we do wrong? What did we neglect to do that we should have done? How did we fail as parents?" Most of us are so accustomed to looking for causes that it is hard to accept the fact that some things just happen. If we knew the cause, we think we could explain the event, and perhaps reverse it.

Living as we do in an age of wondrous technological developments and scientific achievement, we have come to believe that if we are knowledgeable enough and skilled enough, then surely self-interest will fuel willpower enough to cause us to act with good will, and any problems can be solved. So if we discover we have cancer or if we fail in our projects or those we trust turn on us, we begin to think of sins of commission and omission. Then we begin to play the game of "If Only I Had. . . ."

But then we note that the suffering seems far out of proportion to any sin that might have been committed, and worse yet that not all persons seem to suffer equally from similar sins.

Hundreds of people went to the Hyatt Regency Hotel in Kansas City to celebrate many things in this newest and most luxurious of hostelries. At one time or another most of them were under the skywalk. Only some were there when the skywalks fell in 1982. Over a hundred were killed. Some were crippled for life. Some were injured but recovered. Some were shaken but not hurt.

If there is little evidence that the victim has committed a sin grave enough to warrant such suffering or has failed to do what might have prevented it, then some argue that either he or she did something wrong in another incarnation, as in the Hindu concept, or else the sins of the fathers are visited on the children. This latter view is sometimes expressed in the Bible.

This too has some plausibility when we see that pregnant mothers who use drugs may give birth to malformed or drug addicted babies. Battered children, if they survive, often grow up to be battering parents. Persons who have been deeply hurt seem to pass along the hurt.

In spite of some plausibility, however, it violates our sense of fair play to assume that God would deliberately design a world in which innocent persons would be made to suffer for what others have done.

Related to this concept of suffering as a result of sin is the one that sees the individual as caught up in the body of a people or tribe so that a whole nation can be made to suffer for the sins of some of its members. The Old Testament prophets frequently pointed to drought, to pestilence, and to defeat in war as punishment for disobedience to God's commandments. Invading armies intent on pillage and in pursuit of power were seen to be scourges of God; they carried on their ravages and maintained their oppression by the will of God for the purpose of cleansing a nation from its sins and directing its people back to obedience. On the other side, God promised Lot he would spare the cities of Sodom and Gomorrah if Lot could find ten righteous men. So while a whole people might be punished for the sins of some, a people might also be redeemed by the holiness of a remnant.

Although it is hard for those of us who have been taught more individualistic notions of responsibility to accept this point of view, there is a sense in which a whole people do suffer, just as a group is blessed by the work of some of its members. The sins of one do have repercussions that affect all. For example, one of the common violations of trust in our time is theft, all the way from petty pilfering to major embezzlement and wholesale fraud. It has been estimated that as much as 15% of the cost of health care is due to stealing. A deeper cost is the inconvenience it causes in the care of the ill, which causes the quality of care to deteriorate. A still deeper cost is that it breaks the bonds of trust that hold a community together.

People refuse to wear helmets when they ride motorcycles or to buckle seat belts when they drive. It is inconvenient, they say. They are careful, they claim. Besides, it is their own business if they want to take risks with their own lives and persons. However, if they are injured or crippled, all of us bear part of the costs of medical care, increased insurance rates, and the loss of productivity. Human life is made more difficult by everything from the practice of incivility, such as using two parking spaces in a crowded parking lot, and discourtesy to those who wait on us or to those whom we wait on, to the terrorism endemic in modern warfare in which innocent bystanders suffer the most.

Why would God create a world in which persons do such terrible things to themselves and to each other? Why do the worst of us seem to get away with murder, so to speak, while the best of us sometimes bear a load of trouble and pain?

Some of the answer may be found in the Christian affirmation that God created humankind in his own image, making humans just a little lower than the angels. This means that because we have the capacity to create, we also have the power to destroy. This means that we are created with a consciousness that enables us to be aware of our own frailty in a dangerous world and of our eventual death. We are created with a memory that enables us to relive hurts and narrow escapes over and over again, and by an imagination that enables us to visualize all the dreadful things that may happen in the future. This means we are created also with the freedom to make choices about what we will do and what kinds of persons we will become. With freedom comes responsibility. With responsibility comes suffering when freedom is misused in the process of learning how to be human.

All animate, sensate creatures react to pain or to a strong stimulus that signals danger and causes them to try to evade the source of the pain. The higher animals, at least, learn to associate pain with certain situations. However, animals do not seem to worry about pain before it comes, and they do not seem to fret about it after it is over. And in most living creatures there is a mechanism that seems to anesthetize the victim after injury.

Human beings suffer not only from the pain but also from anxiety, from fear of being hurt, from guilt, from loneliness and alienation. The myth of the fall speaks to the relationship between learning the difference between good and evil, the loss of innocence, and suffering engendered by human sin.

Reinhold Niebuhr has described sin as being rooted in the anxiety engendered by our awareness of our own finiteness and mortality.[2] On the one hand, we try to escape from the anxiety by denying or repressing the awareness of our vulnerability. So we struggle to make ourselves secure, even if others have to be pushed aside or put out of the way. We seek to amass wealth, power, and learning so we will not need to be dependent on anyone. We seek immortality by making a name for ourselves and leaving monuments to our greatness. So we deny our humanness and try to be gods.

On the other hand, we try to submerge our anxiety in sensuality, deadening our awareness by frenetic activity or by using narcotics. So we deny our humanness by surrendering to animality.

In either case we inflict injury upon ourselves and others, often in willful defiance of what we know to be good, as well as from ignorance and stupidity. So we recognize that much of the suffering and evil in the world comes as the result of the misuse of human freedom either on our part or on that of others. This is the price we pay for being part of a community.

But then we note that there is evil in the world that seems to have little to do with human decision or activity. Floods, droughts, earthquakes, volcanic eruptions, lightning, and disease come of their own accord and strike at random.

God allows suffering for a purpose

It is a small step from the recognition that we bring pain on ourselves or on others through the misuse of freedom, which is what makes us human, to a conviction that suffering must have some purpose. It is easy to see that pain exists to remind us that we are in danger and need to take steps to avoid or overcome the danger. We feel the heat of the flame and draw away lest we be burned up entirely. We begin to ache and realize that we are being told we must change our behavior. So pain can be looked on as a warning bell and as an incentive to correct courses of action.

Suffering also has been described by some as a pedagogue to teach us our limits and to prevent us from destroying ourselves. It is said to be a training ground on which we can develop strength of character, acquire patience, learn compassion, and develop bonds of empathy with others. Paul says,

> we also rejoice in our sufferings, because we know that suffering produces perseverance; perseverance produces character; and character, hope. And hope does not disappoint us, because God has poured out his love into our hearts by the Holy Spirit, whom has been given to us (Rom. 5:3-4).

We should note here, however, that it is not the suffering that is doing this, but the Holy Spirit, who enables Paul to make use of the suffering.

Paul is not talking about the suffering that comes from mistakes made out of ignorance or the negative consequences of his own sin, but of the evil encountered in the course of human existence. My wife and I have learned that the experiences of having a child handicapped by deafness and a sister crippled by polio, as well as close encounters with cancer, Parkinson's disease, and Alzheimer's disease, have given us an understanding of others who go through such trials that we would not have had before and have brought us into contact with gallant, courageous people who have enriched our own lives.

In the book of Job we are introduced to the idea that Job's suffering was allowed by God, if not caused by God, in order to test his faith and to see if he was worthy of the trust placed in him. And yet it would seem that an all-knowing God would not need to go to such cruel lengths to be assured of Job's integrity, nor would he be so cavalier as to put one of his creatures through such an ordeal just to win a bet with the devil.

I think of several persons who were mentors of mine when I was beginning on my career, persons whom I came to love and respect deeply and who lived exemplary lives if anyone can. Now in their ninth decade, they have become exceedingly frail and able to move only with help. One especially is limited also by failing eyesight. Having lost his wife of many years, he now lives alone. When I visited with them, I could not help but shake my head in anger and regret over the ruin of their bodies by the ravages of time. I cannot believe that their suffering is the will of God, although they may serve God's purpose in spite of and through their suffering.

The youngest child of a friend of mine was born with Down's syndrome. The father says that although they grieved over this at first, this has proved to be one of God's greatest gifts to their family. I am sure they did transform the situation by their love into something good.

It is impossible for me to believe that it is the will of God, who is all-powerful and all-loving, for children to be born deformed or to be crippled by disease or accident just to learn how to be loving. It does not square with my understanding of God as revealed in Jesus Christ to believe that it is his will that people have cancer or arthritis, any more than he wills that some persons should be exploited, abused, oppressed, or betrayed by other human beings. Such a God would be more like a capricious and unfeeling despot than a loving and dependable father. But at the same time, if we hold that God is the creator of the universe, and if there is evil in that universe, then in some way he has to be assigned some of the responsibility for it. So suffering must have some meaning.

The devil did it

Because we do not want to blame God for the evil in the world, and because blaming God does not square with the affirmation of his absolute goodness and unconditional love, Christians often have been drawn toward the Manichaean heresy of seeing reality as divided more or less equally between two separate powers; life is a warfare between the forces of darkness and the forces of light. From this point of view demonic, destructive forces preexist and coexist with the angelic, creative forces with which they conflict. God confronts Satan, the Prince of Darkness, who is responsible for all evil and who constantly tries to draw each of us into his evil network, not only working evil on us but also inveigling us into doing his work by causing evil. This view too can be found in the Bible.

Early people saw the world as populated with evil spirits lurking behind every stone and tree. Their lives were filled with dread. Their days were occupied in placating these spirits or by walking carefully, following endless rituals to avoid disturbing or irritating them. As humankind became more sophisticated, it conceived of these evil spirits as organized in a hierarchy under a supreme ruler of darkness. God has his legions of angels. Satan has his legions of demons working for him. It is the latter that pressure us and tempt us to do wrong, that lead us into blind alleys, and that heap troubles on our heads. All we can do is to ally ourselves with the good and resist the evil with all our might.

Too often this viewpoint has led to scapegoating, for it is too easy to identify those whom we do not like or do not know or fear as agents of the Enemy, who are to be ruthlessly extirpated in a holy war. That which is within us can too easily be projected outward as a way of shifting the blame on someone else.

We also have to admit that we sometimes feel as if we have been caught up in the grip of forces of evil beyond our control. There seem to be situations in which we can do no other than wrong. The writer of the letter to the Ephesians says,

> For our struggle is not against flesh and blood, but against the rulers, against the authorities, against the powers of this dark world and against the spiritual forces of evil in the heavenly realms (Eph. 6:12).

Human sinfulness has become institutionalized in structures of society, in the customs, laws, and cultural patterns in which we are caught up and which cause suffering. Slavery, racism, sexism, imperialism, economic exploitation do exist. These are Frankensteins of human creating that tend to take on a life of their own. These are to be called under the judgment of God, resisted by us with all our might, and changed so that the structures of our social existence more nearly reflect that mind that was in Christ. Not to resist these evils is to be a party to evil.

In the Judeo-Christian tradition the forces of evil are not coexistent with God nor are they coequal. Therefore, they eventually will be overcome and brought into subjection to God. The story of the fall of Lucifer transfers the misuse of freedom into the heavenly spheres, holding that even angels rebelled against God and attempted to set themselves up as gods.

The Christian gospel is that God not only is all-powerful and all-good but also that in time all creatures will worship him and do his will. The gospel is that the kingdom of God is here now wherever persons do his will and is in the process of coming with power. The gospel is that if we live by faith in the saving grace of God, we too will enter the kingdom and have the gift of eternal life in spite of our sinfulness, and in spite of our sufferings we will be transformed.

The book of Job makes Satan responsible for Job's troubles—his boils, the loss of his wealth, the death of his children. But Satan does what he does with God's permission. He can go only as far as God will allow him to go. And he is allowed to do his work for a purpose. So in a sense this still makes God responsible for the presence of evil in the world. Many questions remain unanswered.

Our number comes up

Another approach abandons the idea of a universe created by a God who has a purpose in creating and thus gives meaning to human existence. It abandons also the idea that human existence and the universe are a battleground between opposing forces. This approach adopts the idea that we live in a world governed only by the laws of chance and probability or by an inexorable fate.

According to this view, disease and death and calamity come when the wheel of fortune stops on our number. In the presence of extreme danger, as in battle, persons often take a fatalistic approach, shrug their shoulders and say, "If my number comes up I will die. If not I will live. There is nothing I can do to change the odds very much."

In a sense this view holds that there is no meaning either in suffering or not suffering. The only meaning is to be found in deciding to live as well as we can or not to live and commit suicide.

To hold this view consistently is to see ourselves as completely imbedded in nature, subject to impersonal laws governing that nature. We participate in the cycles of spinning atoms.

But it is clear that we are not completely at the mercy of the operation of natural laws and cycles of the seasons. Because of our intelligence we can act to change the way in which we are affected by events around us. We can tilt the pinball machine. It is only when we are completely trapped in situations in which we seem to have no choice that we seem to be pawns of chance. Even then we can decide what kinds of pawns we will be, even if we cannot decide where we will be moved.

Evil is a mystery

In the final analysis, when we have said all we can, there is still much about this world that is absurd, much we cannot explain. Suffering remains an unfathomable mystery.

The book of Job opens bravely with the disclosure that Job's suffering was caused by the devil, with God's consent, in order to test Job's faith and enable God to win a bet. This provided the occasion for Job's so-called friends to trot out all the cliches about suffering, such as "Surely you must have sinned to warrant such suffering," as if these would be of comfort. It also gave them an opportunity to flaunt their superiority as having avoided suffering.

But the book ends with a catalog of mysteries. God himself takes the podium with a list of unanswerable questions. "Where were you when I laid the earth's foundation? . . . Can you bind the beautiful Pleiades? Can you loose the cords of Orion?" (Job 38:4,31). Volley after volley of questions comes until Job admits, "I know you can do all things; no plan of yours can be thwarted" (Job 42:2). After we have acknowledged our part in it through ignorance and sin, suffering is a mystery to be endured with as much gallantry and courage as we can muster.

The New Testament does not have an explanation for suffering. It only proclaims that God is in charge of his world and that a time will come when all suffering will cease, all tears will be dried, and all sorrow swallowed up in laughter. Then all things will be made clear, and the balances of justice will be redressed. God wills our salvation and our fulfillment, not our suffering or our destruction. God wills healing, not hurt. God wills eternal life, not death.

In the meantime, the world is filled with what the theologian John Macquarrie calls "loose ends."[3] The tragic pervades human existence. We bring suffering on ourselves. We cause others to suffer out of ignorance or malevolence. We often can choose only between two evils. The wheel of chance does seem to stop at random, bringing devastation in its wake for some and good fortune to others. The disorder is that of the artist's studio or the mechanic's workshop. It is a part of the messiness of the creative process, the debris wrought in the completing of the universe.

In *Creation and Chaos* Bernhard Anderson reminds us that in the Genesis story God created by imposing order upon a primeval, watery chaos.[4] The Exodus story shows God making a people out of a disorganized rabble of outcasts and slaves. Again and again in the Old Testament there is a consciousness that this chaos may break loose again.

We can experience this chaos in the sudden upsurge of greed when we are presented with a can't-fail-get-rich scheme, or in an outbreak of sexual longing when we meet another who awakens something deep within us, or in an outburst of rage when pressed too hard and too long. When these happen, homes and relationships and carefully built reputations are sometimes shattered. Contemporary physicists are talking now about chaos underlying order in the universe, making it impossible to predict with accuracy or to control events completely.

Perhaps God himself is growing and learning and changing. Paul wrote:

> For the creation waits in eager expectation for the sons of God to be revealed. For the creation was subjected to frustration, not by its own choices, but by the will of the one who subjected it. . . . We know that the whole creation has been groaning as in the pains of childbirth right up to the present time. Not only so, but we ourselves, who have the first fruits of the Spirit, groan inwardly as we wait eagerly for . . . the redemption of our bodies (Rom. 8:19-23).

Perhaps out of the chaos God is continuing his creating, out of the struggle working to bring all to completion and to perfection.

The finite mind cannot see earthquake, famine, malaria, polio, cancer, and the aging process from the infinite perspective. We can know only that we are a part of a world in the making. We have been given an opportunity to participate in that making, to be involved in the sweat and pain and muck of the cosmic project.

God is in it with us

In Christ we see God participating fully in the agony of creation along with all of his creatures, demonstrating the power to accept suffering as part of the creative process, choosing suffering as part of the price of loving and redeeming, and transcending suffering in the resurrection. For Christians the cross has come to be the ultimate symbol of suffering and of death, and at the same time of suffering and death transcended and transformed. The cross was laid on Jesus by others. But the cross was also accepted by Jesus when it could have been avoided, used to witness to humankind about the power of love and forgiveness. In Jesus we see God himself undergoing crucifixion on behalf of his creatures.

The spectacle of the sinless one tortured and killed by those whom he had come to save is the ultimate paradigm of suffering in the world. We are filled with rage and sorrow that it could happen. We want to take revenge on those who did it, only to find ourselves implicated in the continuing crucifixions among humankind. Then we are humbled and broken by the majesty of the love and forgiveness demonstrated there. There we learn how to face our own suffering and death, putting ourselves into the hands of God.

James Russell Lowell expressed the truth of this paradigm when he wrote as he agonized over the issue of human slavery:

Truth forever on the scaffold,
Wrong forever on the throne,—
Yet that scaffold sways the future,
And, behind the dim unknown,
Standeth God within the shadow,
Keeping watch above his own.[5]

So I do not know why our son has been deaf since birth or why the residual hearing he had diminished to almost nothing over the years. I do not know why our daughter developed Parkinson's disease at age 30. I do not know why my wife was afflicted with cancer and had to undergo a mastectomy to save her life. I do not know why among my close friends some died long before their time of heart failure or leukemia. I am baffled by these facts. I hurt to see those I love hurt. I cannot help but feel some anger over their suffering and the losses I have experienced.

Yet these who have suffered have demonstrated the vibrancy of a will to live in spite of all, courage and persistence in making meaningful lives, gallantry in dealing with handicap and loss, and lives lived in faith in the face of uncertainty. All these have enriched my life as they have lived richly in spite of affliction.

Why greed and hatred and cruelty are rampant among humankind, why classes and races and nations clash in internecine war, I do not know. I do know that sacrificial love, unconditional forgiveness, unfailing mercy also exist.

Robert Ingersoll, the 19th-century criminal lawyer, was an agnostic gadfly of the religious establishment. However, in the funeral oration for his beloved brother, he said, "In the night of death, listening love hears the rustle of an angel's wing and hope sees a star."[6]

Zorba the Greek devoted hours of arduous labor to building a device he dreamed up to bring logs down from the top of the mountain to the shore where they could be made into props for his mine.[7] When put into operation, instead of working as he thought it would, it collapsed. Months of work went down the drain. When the dust had settled, he calmly ate the feast prepared to celebrate his anticipated success. Then he went to the seashore and danced until he was exhausted. Perhaps all we can do in such times is to dance or to sing until we see that God sings and dances with us.

An opportunity for ministry

Even though suffering remains a mystery and we can come up with only partially satisfying explanations for the existence of evil in the world, suffering does present us with opportunity to demonstrate the mercy and love of God and to engage in the redemptive ministry of Jesus Christ. His disciples pointed to the man who had been blind from birth and challenged Jesus: "Who sinned, this man or his parents, that he was born blind?" The reply of Jesus was, "Neither this man nor his parents sinned, but this happened so that the work of God might be displayed in his life" (John 9:1-3).

This was an occasion for compassion, not condemnation. It was an opportunity for demonstrating loving care, not hairsplitting argument. Without the night, sunshine would be taken for granted. Without black, painting could have no depth. Without suffering in this world, we would have no occasion for the shining saga of heroic deeds of mercy and feats of healing performed on behalf of others.

Consider the meaning and purpose given to the lives of those who seek the cure and prevention of disease or who care for those who have become dependent. Consider the significance of those who pursue peace and justice in the world, who work to reduce crime and violence, who take great risks to rescue those who have fallen into peril. Consider also those who try to organize to see that no one starves and to find new sources of food so that no one goes hungry. Consider those who work to prevent floods and droughts by taming and harnessing water-ways. Even those who are wasting away with a terminal illness can at least demonstrate to those who come after how to die.

Coping with Pain and Suffering

When we sustain a permanent, serious loss, when we are afflicted with a disease that cannot be cured and which may grow progressively worse, when we experience continual pain, or when we suffer emotionally and psychologically from what has happened to persons close to us, how do we cope? We might even ask how we can preserve some measure of serenity when we are bombarded on every side by the news media with tales of corruption, chicanery, and catastrophe.

It is very easy to begin to feel persecuted and sorry for ourselves, to be filled with constant anger vented on everyone who comes near us, or to be a chronic complainer. It is easy to become cynical about life and people. It is tempting to give way to despair and to give up or to decide that life has no meaning.

Neither Christian faith nor righteous living nor fervent prayer can assure us that we will not fall victims to suffering. In the early days of my ministry I read the funeral rites for a young mother who died from cancer, leaving four small children. Her husband was distraught and inconsolable. His faith was shattered. He said, "Both of us have been regular members of the church all our lives. We tried to do what is right. We tithed. We have been taught that if we had faith and prayed long enough, we could have what we needed. When we learned that Marion had cancer, we prayed that she might be spared long enough to raise the children. We didn't think that was selfish or unreasonable. But now she is dead. I no longer believe there is a God. Or if there is a God who would let this happen, I don't want anything to do with him."

The young husband should not have been taught so simplistically. Jesus himself prayed in the garden that he be spared the agony of the cross. On the cross he struggled with the feeling that God had abandoned him. But at last he was able to say, "Father, into your hands I commit my spirit" (Luke 23:46).

Faith does enable persons to withstand and surmount tragedy and hurt. Prayer does fortify the spirit and assuage the pain. Healing does come to some in ways that seem miraculous. Some are saved from earthquake, fire, flood, shipwreck, airplane crash, kidnappers, and concentration camp in ways that seem like the answer to prayer. But not all of us who pray with equal fervor are spared. Some of us will not be able to go around the fire. We will have to go through it in spite of our prayers.

Accept the evil as a fact

We can begin by accepting the reality of the loss and the limitations we sustain by acknowledging the pain as well as the fear and anger we may feel. If we try to pretend the situation does not exist, to repress consciousness of it and of our feelings, or to increase our efforts to go on as if nothing has happened, we keep ourselves from being able to cope with it most creatively.

If we can admit our vision is going, we can wear glasses, use more light, get a magnifying lens, and try to use our ears more. If our hearing is going, we can sit up front near the speaker; we can ask persons to speak more loudly or repeat what we did not catch; we can use hearing aids and try to pay more attention to visual cues of communication. If we are physically limited or disabled, we can use canes, walkers, or wheelchairs to get around. Pride and vanity, which lead us to deny our affliction, may keep us from making use of resources that would increase our freedom.

Rejoice in what is good

While we accept the reality of the evil we experience, we can recall with gratitude the good we have known in the past and rejoice in whatever degree of health, companionship, freedom, and power that is left to us in the present. Paul knew suffering at first hand. His letter to the Philippians, addressed to persons under pressure of persecution, gives counsel that is still sound:

> Rejoice in the Lord always. I will say it again: Rejoice! Let your gentleness be evident to all. The Lord is near. Do not be anxious about anything, but in everything by prayer and petition, with thanksgiving, present your requests to God (Phil. 4:4-6).

Focus on your resources

It helps to remember the measure of freedom that is left to us to decide and to act, the powers we still possess to accomplish what we need to, and the resources available to us, rather than to dwell on the loss and the pain. It helps to think about

the deeds of loving kindness performed daily by persons every-
where, of sacrificial lives lived on behalf of others, and of
great works of beauty that have been accomplished. As Paul
wrote to the Philippians:

> . . . whatever is true, whatever is noble, whatever is right,
> whatever is pure, whatever is lovely, whatever is admirable—
> if anything is excellent or praiseworthy—think about such things
> (Phil. 4:8).

We can strive to appreciate beauty of nature and of art more,
to cultivate a sense of humor so we can laugh more. In the
last few years I have found enjoyment and insight in the study
of biography and poetry.

Think about others

When a woman asked whether she should seek psychiatric
help when she felt depressed, Karl Menninger is reported to
have told her she should put on her hat and coat, go out of the
house, close the door behind her, and find someone else who
was in need to care for. Those who have been through a crisis
can be more helpful to others going through a crisis than those
who have not. Helping others is one way to gain balance on
one's own affliction.

One of the persons who greatly inspired me was a woman
in her middle years who was badly crippled, confined to a
wheelchair, and in great pain from rheumatoid arthritis. She
kept a telephone on a table beside her wheelchair and beside
the telephone a card file with the names, telephone numbers,
and birthdays or anniversaries of several hundred persons she
knew. Every day she went through her file and called those
who had a birthday or other anniversary to wish them well.

Avoid a cult of suffering

There is no virtue in suffering in itself. We should not seek out suffering. When it comes, we should not make it the center of our lives. We should not use it to manipulate others or to make ourselves the center of attention.

Facing the Fear of Dependency

With modern medicine pain is not the problem it once was, for we now have ways of controlling pain. What we fear is becoming dependent on others, the loss of control over our bodily functions, and the possibility of losing our cognitive and rational faculties. We fear the fall of the self into limbo while we await the slow and tardy arrival of death. At one point my mother forgot that it was Mother's Day and that we had arranged to take her out for dinner. She was embarrassed and said, "I guess I'm going crazy." She also admitted that this scared her.

Another factor is feelings of guilt about being not only useless but also a burden on others. When all our adult lives we have been expected and have expected ourselves to be strong and caring and capable, earning our own keep, standing on our own two feet, solving our problems on our own, we don't want to be a problem to others. This is made even worse if we deeply care about others and assume that our dependency is going to put them under stress. We may also fear that they will begin to resent us.

Still another factor is the fear that in our dependency we will be totally in the hands of strangers. We live in a society where many of our relationships are instrumental rather than organic, where transactions between persons are limited to specific functions, and where persons help each other in return for pay. So we may fall into the hands of strangers who will not know what we have been or who we are now, and whose care is given for pay rather than out of filial duty or love.

We need to examine our attitude toward dependency. Perhaps we have overdone our teaching about being independent and have placed too high a value on it. Perhaps we need to learn more about being interdependent and about being dependent when that is appropriate. We do not resent the dependency of children, and although children may be concerned about powerlessness, generally they do not resent being dependent. As they grow older, they do seek to gain a greater degree of control over their own lives and to be freed from some restrictions on their movements. Babies are frail and need to be cared for totally, to be bathed, fed, and have their diapers changed. They are valued for themselves alone more than for their potential as adult producers and continuations of the family line. Why do we find frailty and dependence in the old disgusting?

Sally Godow said:

> Physical frailty is simply one of the colors an existence will have, and an especially strong color at that. . . . Frailty is defined as the degree to which one's intensity can find expression. It is an intense experience and brings with it new life. . . . Frailty is at once a limit and a freedom.[8]

We do have problems in our society with frailty and with the care of those who have become dependent. Some of these problems are rooted in values, attitudes, and social expectations. Some are rooted in the lack of institutions and facilities to support persons who are frail. But each of us has to come to grips with the prospect or the experience of being frail, disabled, or dependent. How shall we do this?

All our lives we have been somewhat dependent on others, at some times more than others. This is what it means to be a human being. Perhaps we have borne our fair share of responsibility for the care of others who might have been dependent on us. Thus we begin by acknowledging our interdependence upon each other and our need to be interdependent.

All our lives we have had to work within physical limitations. We have had to learn how to make the best of the strength and ability given to us at any stage in our life. We have had to work to enhance these abilities, both to enlarge and to keep from losing them. We have had to find our freedom within these limits, no matter what our fantasies might have been or how much we might have regretted not being more talented. We have had to accept the fact that we cannot expect ourselves to go beyond those limits and so have been relieved of responsibility for trying.

As our waning strength and diminishing physical capacity reduce the area of our freedom, we can still seek ways to enhance and to use to the full our remaining abilities. To live within these limits without fretting we have to learn to reduce the expectations we place on ourselves and to relinquish our fantasies about doing more or being more.

I confess that I do not know how I might feel or how I might react if I found myself in a situation where the most appropriate care for me would be found in a nursing home and I would be called on to make the decision to enter such a home. I say, "enter" rather than "allow myself to be put" in a nursing home. We do not say we are "put" in an acute hospital. We go to a hospital, even though reluctantly and fearfully, because that is the place where we can receive treatment most commensurate with our physical condition out of all the alternate kinds of placement. I am "put" in a nursing home only when my caretakers have exhausted all other resources and I am unwilling to accept the fact or when I have become incompetent to decide.

So I can either enter this, like any other situation, figuratively kicking and screaming, which would only injure myself and others, or I can go cooperatively with faith and hope. I can go resenting others whom I judge to have abandoned me and in fear of those who are to care for me, or I can go with gratitude toward those who have been caring for me and in faith that the Holy Spirit will be working through those who are to care for me. Probably I would have a mixture of these feelings. But I pray I might have faith enough to take the positive approach.

This requires me to remember that my basic worth comes from the fact that I am one whom God loves so much that he sent his only Son so that I might be saved and given new life. In Christ we see God reaching across pain-filled gulfs, reconciling us to each other and all of us to him. God is in it with us, even on a cross. He suffers, too, as his Spirit moves over the troubled waters of chaos to bring order. He will go with us into the nursing home. Even within the confines of a nursing home, we are called to join with God in the process of ordering that creation. We can make a difference, even though we have to make it within a smaller area of freedom.

It is in the light of that knowledge that we can join with Paul and Silas in singing, even at midnight, in the darkest hour of our lives, while we wait for the doors of the prison to open and the daylight to dawn.

CHAPTER FIVE

Listen for Your Calling

We older people often complain that we are of no use any more. No one needs us. There is nothing we can do. We might as well be dead, because we are only a care and a burden on others. We see retirement as being laid on the shelf or put out to pasture. We often experience it as rejection.

After I retired, somewhat to my surprise I found myself a little embarrassed to write "retired" in the blanks asking about occupation and employer. I was not altogether sure I wanted to be numbered among those who were no longer producing. The word seemed to imply that I was cut off from those who were doing important things. Finally I solved the problem by writing "self-employed."

One day, before my retirement, I called on a 94-year-old resident in a nursing home. Grace Dillingham was frail but alert. Before she retired she had a distinguished career as a teacher in Korea under her denomination's board of missions. With great pride she showed me pictures of the large, well-known school she had built in a Korean city. She showed me pictures of her students and told me about many who had gone on to become outstanding leaders in Korea.

For nearly four decades she had been a considerable influence in the development of that country. Later in the conversation she told me that she no longer had any reason to live. She hoped she would die soon. Her work was finished. Her body was no longer able to respond to the command of her spirit. There was nothing more for her to do. Life was no longer worth living.

We can understand. Believing that one's worth depends on being able to do something or produce something is a typical American attitude. Obviously her life was drawing to a close after a long retirement. But what of the days left for her to live? What on earth are old people good for anyway? Or, to use stronger language, more descriptive of a felt condition and with theological overtones, "What in hell are older people supposed to do with themselves?"

Each of us needs a goal and a purpose in life. We need to survive, but we also need something to make life worth living. Survival is not enough. When there is nothing to live for, we die.

In his book *Man's Search for Meaning*, Viktor Frankl, a Viennese psychiatrist, describes how he lived through the hell of Nazi concentration camps.[1] He saw his mother, father, wife, and children go into the gas chambers. He himself nearly died more than once from starvation and typhus. He testified that those who survived did so because they were able to find and to commit themselves to a purpose, to the pursuit of some value that gave meaning to their existence in the death camps.

Bronislaw Malinowski, the pioneer anthropologist, in his classic work *Argonauts of the Western Pacific*, described the life and culture of the Trobriand islanders.[2] In the main their life was easy, because the climate provided an abundance of food with a minimum of effort and reduced to almost nothing

the need for clothing and shelter. Their island habitat protected
them from raids by enemies. This left them with time on their
hands, which they used to equip and organize expeditions to
far-off islands to trade for strings of beads made from certain
kinds of seashells. These expeditions, often requiring months
for planning and preparation, were surrounded with religious
rites and ceremonies. The shells occupied a place in their economy not too different from that of diamonds, pearls, or the
crown jewels in ours. Then Western explorers found the islands
and called into question the value of what the people were
doing. After the islanders lost faith in their system of values
because a stronger people ridiculed what they did, they seemed
to lose their will to live, and they began to die out.

In October 1982, a consultation was held with 48 older
Christians representing a cross section of their denomination.
They were asked, "What do you expect from your church?"
They strongly asserted that they did not want to be cared for,
but rather they wanted to be given opportunities to be in ministry. They wanted to be involved, to be empowered for significant social roles.

Answers to the question of what on earth are we good for
may be found in the Christian teaching about vocation or calling. This puts the questions in transcendent perspective and
rephrases them: What does God intend for me to be and to do
with my life? What is my calling now that I am in my 70s and
retired? What is my vocation now that I am in a nursing home?

The Doctrine of Vocation

The doctrine of vocation is corollary to the doctrine of creation. In the creation story humans were commissioned to
till and to keep the garden that God had brought into being.
In the story of the patriarchs Abraham was called out of Haran

to enter a land and found a nation. Moses was called to go back into Egypt to lead his people out of slavery. The Hebrews as a people were called to occupy a land and to keep it for their descendants.

In his letter to the Romans the apostle Paul shares his conviction that

> . . . in all things God works for the good of those who love him, who have been called according to his purpose. For those God foreknew he also predestined to be conformed to the likeness of his Son, that he might be the firstborn among many brothers. And those he predestined, he also called; those he called, he also justified; those he justified, he also glorified (Rom. 8:28-30).

The writer of the letter to the Ephesians put it similarly:

> For he chose us in him before the creation of the world to be holy and blameless in his sight (Eph. 1:4).

Here both fulfillment and glorification are rooted in responsiveness to God's calling. God intends that our lives be fulfilled and glorified through participation with Christ not only in the creation but also the redemption of the world.

These letters were written to congregations of persons. The early Christians took the Greek word *ekklesia* to describe their congregations. In ancient Greece the *ekklesia* was the gathering of the free citizens of a city who were called together by the herald. Christians were given their freedom and made citizens of the kingdom of God by virtue of their calling into the fellowship of Christ. It was this calling that gave meaning to their lives.

The charter for this calling is to be found in two statements. One is the Great Commandment to love the Lord our God with all our being and to love our neighbors as ourselves. The other is the Great Commission to go into all the world and to make disciples of all nations.

All or only a few?

There are those who have questioned whether everyone is intended to be saved or only a select few. Are all called to love God, or only some special persons? The question arises because it is obvious that some have been given the opportunity to hear the gospel and to experience love while others have not. It is clear also that among those who hear, some respond and others do not. The book of Exodus states that Pharaoh's refusal to let the Hebrews go was because God had hardened Pharaoh's heart. Did God deliberately set Pharaoh and all the Egyptians up for destruction?

Certainly it is a mystery why we have been the ones who have heard the proclamation of the good news and have been invited to participate in the body of Christ while others have not. This is a cause for humble gratitude; to swell with pride about receiving God's grace would be to negate it. It is hard to understand why some who have been shown love do not or cannot respond with love and do not mold their lives according to the mind of Christ. We need to be cautious about making judgments that only God can make about the status and experience of others. We can only affirm that it is God's intention that each and every human being walk with him in love, doing justly and loving mercy because God loves all that he has made. With John we hold that God so loved the world (not just parts of it) that he sent his only Son, that whosoever believes in him might have life and have it abundantly.

All to be ministers?

Are we all called to be ministers of Christ, or only a few? There are those who do not believe that everyone is called by God in the sense of being commissioned to a life of ministry. The teaching about Christian vocation has been distorted by elitism and sacerdotalism to mean that some occupations are sacred, and persons are called to them, while other occupations are profane, and persons merely fall into them or else choose them out of prudential considerations. The clergy are set off from the laity as "religious," and the work of the other Christians is thought of as secular or worldly. So some believe God's work is limited to priestly activities carried on by a few; all the others do mundane things with little or no ultimate significance. This has the effect of trivializing much of what they do.

Related to this concept is the thought that we worship God only in specially sanctified places such as church buildings. So in addition to devaluing most of the world's work, we ignore the presence of the holy in the marketplace, the field, the factory, the school, or the home. The Pharisees fell into this trap by defining holiness in terms of keeping laws; most of those who did the world's work found it impossible to keep the law because of their occupations. It was especially to these "sinners" outside the law that Jesus preached. Ministry is not just doing church work.

Each of us is called to love God and our neighbors wherever we are and in whatever we are doing. We are all called to participate with Christ in carrying out God's creative and redemptive work. We were ordained to the ministry through our baptism at the time we entered into the congregation of the faithful.

Once in our lives?

Are we called once in our lives to a particular vocation?

There are those who think of calling as a once-and-for-all event to a lifelong occupation.

Calling is not to be thought of as a mandate to pursue a lifelong career in some specific occupation. We may change positions in terms of our occupation. We may change careers during a lifetime, as situations change. So our call consists of daily marching orders rather than an initiation into a guild from which we may never be released. It means that there is no part-time as opposed to full-time Christian vocations, although there may be occupations that run counter to the purposes of God. There is no retirement from our calling, even though we may retire from a specific occupation. We are called to "love God and to enjoy him forever."

In one sense, of course, we may speak about God calling us to a specific activity, whether it be remunerated labor or volunteer service, whether in a profession or simply in a relationship such as marriage or parenthood, whether it be as clergy or lay person, for a specific period of time. I have seen myself as called to be a student, a parish pastor, a husband and father, a teacher, an agency staff member, and the administrator of a retirement home. I have seen these all as being in ministry.

How are we called?

How does God reveal his call for us? In some instances God's calling and providence may be discerned only in the patterns we see as we look back. God's calling may come through the abilities given us. It may come through the needs presented to us and to which we can respond. It may come through opportunities opening or doors closing before us. It may come from our own sense of what is right in a particular situation. It may come through what others in the Christian community ask us to do or encourage us to do.

Calling is a dynamic process that flows out of a constant conversation between us and God—changing, developing, unfolding, a cloud that goes before us by day, a pillar of fire that hangs over us by night.

As a young woman with a keen mind and a deep sense of responsibility, as well as a yearning for adventure and an interest aroused by her experience, Grace Dillingham accepted a call to become a missionary. She was commissioned by her church to spread the gospel throughout Korea as a teacher and educational administrator. She played her role for a time on a large stage before a large audience. As the resident of a nursing home with diminished strength she was called to witness to the love of Christ on a much smaller but no less significant stage to a much smaller but no less valuable audience. I stood by her bed on the morning she died. I saw the tears in the eyes of the nurse who closed her eyelids. She had been good for something there far beyond her awareness. She needed to be reminded that a nursing home, too, is a field for mission. By what she was in relation to others in the nursing home, she was participating in the creation of the "Community of the New Being," to use Tillich's words. I believe the problem was that no one had told her how much she was valued as she was.

Another friend, Alice Weed, who also spent her life as a missionary, led a much more zigzag career, which took her from teaching in a Native American school in South Dakota to service in west China until she was driven out by the Communists. She went to Costa Rica as a missionary, then in retirement served as interim pastor of a Hispanic congregation in Los Angeles. Now a resident in a retirement home in Dallas, she has had a book written about her life, the proceeds from which she contributes to missions.[3]

Called to be holy

Just as all are called to be saved and called to be in mission, so all are called to be holy. The First Letter of Peter puts it this way:

As obedient children, do not conform to the evil desires you had when you lived in ignorance. But just as he who called you is holy, so be holy in all you do, since it is written "Be holy, because I am holy" (1 Peter 1:14-16).

God is holy. We are to be like God, to have in us the mind that was in Christ Jesus. We are called to *be someone* as well as to *do something.*

To be *holy* is to be "set apart." To be holy is to be committed or to be dedicated to those values that are at the center of all created being. To be holy also means to be "whole" or "healthy." To be holy is to be perfected, to be mature, to become what God intended when he created us.

It is in commitment to God's calling, in allowing ourselves to be set apart for God's ministry, that we are made whole and grow up into that full measure of maturity that was in Christ Jesus. Perhaps instead of using the term *aging,* we should talk about becoming *fully human,* living out the life to which we were destined. We are called to become old.

Becoming Fully Human

Becoming fully human is what we are about, and the process is not completed until we have died. As the acorn realizes its potential to be a mature oak tree before it falls, we can ask, "How can I realize my potential for becoming a mature human being before I too have played out my destiny to the limit?" Sometimes the oak tree stands majestically with only a few live branches as it slowly dies. Sometimes it stands for a time before it falls.

We can identify at least four of the processes that go into being human.

1. We are to be as fully responsible for ourselves as possible in such a way as to keep to a minimum the burden of our care

on others. This includes a responsibility to keep ourselves as well and strong and healthy as possible, to give as well as take.

2. We can make the space we inhabit and the environment that surrounds us as safe, as comfortable, as productive, and as esthetically pleasing as possible. We can express our calling by the way we arrange, use, and care for our space, whether a single room or the ecosphere.

3. We are responsible for sharing with others in fostering a community that enables humankind as well as "our kind" to survive and to develop their innate capacities. Human beings are inescapably social. Without our imbeddedness in a community we could not exist. Without cooperation we would have long since died out.

4. We are responsible for protecting, nurturing, and inducting the younger and the weaker members of society into the community and its culture. The community ultimately must include all human beings. Culture includes all the cultures of all societies. While doing that, we constantly evaluate and remake our community and our culture in the light of God's revelation of himself and his will.

The Meaning of Love

If it is our vocation to love God and our neighbor, what does this mean when lived out in work and retirement, in sickness and in health? How does that give us a reason for living?

What is love?

Love is not just a feeling, not merely liking or approving, or being emotionally stirred by the presence of another. Love is an attitude, a predisposition to act in a positive, constructive way toward the other.

Love is a verb as well as a noun. Love is known by what it does. Love frees. Love trusts. Love creates. Love unifies. Love reconciles. Love heals. Conversely, actions or policies or attitudes that demean, belittle, dehumanize, or debase are not love. That which destroys without an intent to build is not love. Any exploitation, oppression, or injury of others is not love. As H. Richard Neibuhr once put it, love wants the other to be rather than not to be, to be near rather than distant.[4]

Love has to be expressed by concrete acts within the context of specific relationships. For example, what does love require when a spouse has Alzheimer's disease and when his or her care is destroying our own lives? When is it a loving act to assist a person to enter a nursing home? Or what does it mean to be loving when I am a patient in a hospital or a nursing home? What is the loving thing to do when aged parents become unable to care for themselves?

It is difficult to love in specific cases. We may have to balance the claims of one person against those of another, and their needs against our needs. We may have to weigh the short-run good against the long-range consequences of an action. We may have to restrain violence against ourselves as well as against others.

Two elderly sisters live together. The older is becoming very frail and in need of round-the-clock nursing care. The younger sister is trapped into caring for her by the older one's claim that a family member has a duty to care for other members, and by a refusal to consider any alternatives. The younger is being consumed by the thoughtlessness and imperious need of the elder. What is the meaning of love in this situation?

It is not always easy to tell what actions will bring about the results love intends. Nor is it always easy to know what the consequences of such actions will be or are. It is hard to separate our own self-interest from what we do in relation to others. Therefore we have an obligation to be both knowledgeable and intelligent in our loving. We need to be aware of the tangled web of our own motivations.

Since love entails action, it involves decision. Decisions carry risks. Therefore we act as best we can, aware of our limitations, aware of the need for forgiveness, and aware of the need to forgive. To paraphrase Martin Luther, we have to love God and be prepared to sin bravely, depending on God's grace rather than on our merits for our salvation.

Who is my neighbor?

Since Jesus answered this question by telling the parable of the good Samaritan, it is clear that the neighbor is any person we happen to meet and who is in need. Our neighbors are those persons God gives us in our everyday encounters: the person at the checkout counter in the supermarket, the drivers and passengers of the bus we use, the child who lives next door, and the members of our own household. Our neighbors also include those persons with whom we are related but do not know or see, such as the migrant worker who cuts the lettuce we eat. The neighbor includes the enemy whom we are to love; the enemy is anyone who harasses and annoys or upsets us.

My missionary friend was retired from her mission abroad, where she spent many fruitful years. Because of increasing feebleness, she also had to retire from the career of talking to church groups about missions and her experiences as a missionary. She was confined to a nursing home. She had no family except for one sister almost her own age, who lived some distance away. Her neighborhood had shrunk. Those whom God left for her to love were the loyal friends who called on her, the members of the staff of the nursing home who looked after her, and her local church to which she regularly sent an offering out of her small pension. Within this context she was far more dependent on them than they on her, a reversal of the role taken most of her life. Her loving had to be expressed within a small field and in her dependence rather than dominance over those in that field. God works through weakness to make grace abound.

Values That Can Focus and Give Meaning to Life

L ife is worth living only when we can find meaning in what we are doing and in the situation in which we find ourselves. Meaning is to be found by accepting our calling to love God and the neighbor and by committing ourselves to the ministry love requires.

Love is an *ultimate* value. As such it is expressed through *proximate* values. Viktor Frankl suggests that there are three categories of such values: creative values, experiential values, and attitudinal values.[5]

Creative values

Creative values include doing, making, constructing, and organizing. They involve bringing into being that which did not exist before and would not exist if it were not for the creator. They involve imposing some kind of order on that which is chaotic. They include such things as teaching, communicating, painting, writing, sculpting, acting, storytelling, and making music. For most of us, creative values rank highly. It was her work as a missionary that gave meaning to Grace Dillingham's life and made that life worthwhile.

Work and creative values

Since work and occupational roles figure so largely in the pursuit of meaning for so much of our lives, and since retirement has become an accepted social policy, we need to examine further the relationship between work, calling, and retirement.

Some of us, of course, regard work as a curse laid on humankind as punishment for the sin of our first ancestor. It is hard to regard a life of unremitting and often unprofitable toil as a gift. It is hard to wrest a living from arid, rocky, infertile soil, or to endure droughts and plagues, without wishing for release. It is hard to regard routine and often meaningless labor under an unsympathetic management as a blessing. There are times when the most challenging and rewarding work palls. So many of us look forward to retirement as a blessing that for the first time in our lives may free us for our true calling. Unfortunately, many of us find that retirement has plunged us into a vacuum, leaving us at "loose ends." For even if our work is hard and even if it pays very little, work is important to us beyond what we earn or what we achieve.

For one thing, we tend to define who we are by what we do and for whom we work. We introduce ourselves to each other by stating our occupation. Our estimate of ourselves and of others tends to be determined by how an occupation ranks in the social scale. We even get some satisfaction out of letting others know how hard we work and what a tough job we have. Work anchors our identity. Our job gives us a stage on which to act out the meaning of our lives. So to be unemployed or to be retired from work may do more than reduce our income; it may reduce our self-image or shatter our sense of who we are.

For another thing, work yokes us in relationships with others. We often find our friends among those who work with us. We are stimulated by the give and take we experience on the job. From this fellowship we receive confirmation of our worth and the correction of our judgments. The razzing and the banter tell us we are alive. So to be retired from work may mean being cut off from companionship and isolated. We may try to compensate for this by engaging in conversation with clerks at the store, persons in the doctor's office, or strangers on the bus.

Work also provides us with a way of structuring our time. Even when we do not like it very much, our work gives us a place to go, gets us up in the morning, and offers something to do to occupy our minds and engage our energies. We measure our lives by what we have done and what we have yet to do. We keep track of time not only by the seasons of the year but also by the holidays and vacations from work. Retirement renders vacations and holidays pointless. Work gives us something to talk about when it is done.

Finally, to have an occupation, a trade, a craft, or a profession is to be linked with a long tradition from which we derive the language, the tools, and the practices essential to our jobs. The cook who bakes a loaf of bread carries on a practice started centuries ago when one of our forebears slapped a mixture of water and ground cereal on a hot rock. The farmer who plows a field with a tractor is following in the footsteps of the stone-age yeoman who scratched the ground with a crooked stick to give the cereal grass a better bed to sprout in.

That is why many of us, who are retired against our wills and who are struggling to define our lives, say, "I would gladly pay someone to let me work." "I want to be somebody." "I want to count for something."

That is why we should not retire *from* something; we should retire *to* something, to doing that which is genuinely creative and productive of social good. Activity alone will not compensate for the loss of work. Keeping busy at trivial pursuits, or living it up, or going all out for games can be a distraction or a narcotic to take our minds off the emptiness without really satisfying. We need to be involved in the doing of that which is recognized by those whose judgment we respect as productive of value, which gives us something to get up in the morning for, something to look forward to, something to talk about, something to bring us into relation with others. So some of us will keep on working as long as we can.

However, remunerative employment is not the only way for one to pursue creative values. For many, volunteer service provides a good replacement of work with the additional attraction of being done freely and without putting oneself under pressure. Since I retired, the training and consulting for which I am paid and the teaching I do as a volunteer are equally rewarding. I only want to know, "Is it needed? Will it make a difference?" Now work is less and less distinguishable from play. However, workaholics can get themselves overextended in volunteer activities just as they did when they were employed. But when we have said all this, we need to remind ourselves that play is as much a part of living as work.

Experiential values

Experiential values include sensing, appreciating, enjoying, learning, adventuring. After retiring from an outstanding career as the pastor of prestigious churches, Lynn Radcliff became an ardent bird-watcher, among other activities. He spent hours and hours planning for expeditions to the field, observing birds in their natural habitat, extending his list of birds sighted, taking pictures, developing albums, and giving slide lectures. Others find joy in going to museums, attending concerts, traveling. Here the process is far more valuable than the product, although the fashioning of the product causes the pursuit of these values to overlap with creative values and brings pleasure to others.

Play and experiential values

For children play is serious as well as joyous business. Through play children test their capacities and explore their limits. Through play children practice roles they will take when they become mature. They perfect skills needed in coping with their environments. Through play children experiment with behavior.

We are called to love God in our play as well as in our work. Too often we think of play as nonproductive, or even worse, as destructive. But worship is a form of play as we celebrate life and praise God through telling stories, singing songs, making banners, walking in processionals, and reading psalms in unison. Play can be a way of meeting the neighbor. It can be a way of witnessing to our faith.

Many of my generation, who came of age in the Depression years, never learned to swing easily in the exuberance and spontaneity of play. After we came of age, many of us lacked time, money, and energy for play. We were nurtured on the so-called Puritan ethic. We imbibed the notion of self-denial and the postponement of reward. We came to believe that recreation was acceptable mainly to prepare us to work more efficiently and that vacations were allowable only if they increased productivity, rather than being of value in themselves because they express aspects of being not allowed for in our jobs. So it is not easy for us to feel comfortable with a life of play or in the management of leisure.

Often retirement communities are developed around the golf course, the bowling green, the swimming pool, and the clubhouse with its bar and restaurant. They present the image of a resort or spa. They offer escape from noise, smoke, dirt, crime, strangers, and harsh climate. Such communities build on the notion that a life freed from toil and devoted instead to games and parties will yield ultimate satisfaction.

I am told that in one retirement community 25% of the residents use the recreational facilities, but 50% are involved in religious activities. This seems to suggest that there is more to life than games and parties, as enjoyable as they are. Play has most meaning when balanced against work. Some find that the sterility of the protected environment reduces stimulation more than it offers freedom. Of course, many are able to work out a balance between creative and experiential values even in this setting. Perhaps that is an important one.

Play freed from guilt or from the need to prove something, balanced with devotion to meaningful projects, rounds out our lives. Play freed from the nagging concern for survival or from the need to get ahead, to make something of ourselves, or from a drive for security, becomes more enjoyable. Play redeems the present moment.

Play is most rewarding as a counterpoint, a descant in the process of living that has meaning because it is directed to a purpose.

One aspect of play is the process of defining ourselves.

Attitudinal values

Attitudinal values include the development of the self and the determination of what kind of person we will be in relation to the world around us. They include loving, forgiving, waiting, and suffering. They represent the attempt to express the fruits of the Spirit that the apostle Paul talks about: peace, joy, kindness, patience, and so on. There is a sense in which each of us creates a self as we act out the story of our lives.

Jewell Thompson suffered a stroke in her 60s. For the next eight years she was confined to a bed or wheelchair in a nursing home, mentally alert but unable to talk coherently beyond a few words and phrases. During the eight years she was unfailingly cheerful and loving—an inspiration to all who came near.

Finding meaning in attitudinal values

For some of us the pursuit of creative values may be severely limited. For Esther Parks knitting was one of the things she enjoyed most. Eventually she lost her eyesight, but she retained her ability to knit from memory. She made hundreds of knitted articles, which she gave to her friends.

For others of us the pursuit of experiential values may be severely circumscribed, but we still can make an effort to develop within ourselves attitudes that reflect a commitment to the ethic of love. We can decide what kind of person we will be in relation to others and in response to our situation. Our *selves* can become our most important product. Our experience of loss, confinement, or pain can become the battleground on which we hammer out the issues of meaning and put our lives to the test.

Roles We Can Play

The devotion to any of these values tends to become organized around roles we take in the community. Some of the roles open to us in later maturity may be that of *producer, volunteer, celebrator, artist, student, sage,* and *one who waits.* These are foci of energy. They overlap and are not mutually exclusive.

A producer

First, and most obviously, we can go on doing what we have done most of our lives. Homemakers, physicians, writers, artists, musicians, farmers, mechanics, and nurses, as well as salesmen, have kept on working in the careers they pursued all their lives. Perhaps they lighten their load by working fewer hours per week or by selecting those tasks they enjoy more and are still able to accomplish without undue strain. Those who are self-employed can take this path more easily than others. Those in managerial positions or even on-the-line positions in large organizations may not have this choice unless they become consultants or go into a similar business for them-

selves. This role is most satisfying to those who work in occupations that allow a large scope for the expression of personal
needs and abilities.

A volunteer

If one has been freed from the necessity or obligation to
earn an income, a second possibility is to turn to those activities
which one always wanted to get involved in but did not have
that time or opportunity, serving the community as a volunteer.
For one man this took the form of spending almost full time
as a volunteer leader in a social agency, rather than continuing
his former part-time service. For another it was to become
deeply involved in political activities. For another it was to
work seriously on the management of investments and the dis-
bursements of income through philanthropy.

A celebrator

A third way is to expand and enhance that aspect of life
which has been a part of our existence, namely to be an ex-
periencer, a consumer, an enjoyer, and an appreciator of what
others have done or what nature has developed. We may have
time to get acquainted with trees and flowers and birds in the
out-of-doors. We may visit museums and art galleries. We may
watch baseball games. We may go to hear the symphony, to
see plays, and to participate in festivals. Many of these things
are free or inexpensive. Senior citizen discounts are available
to many events and places. We may go dancing, roller-skating,
canoeing, bowling, or golfing.

An artist

A fourth way is to invest our time in artistic creation, to
give esthetically pleasing form and shape to what we see and
know through painting, writing, weaving, sculpture, ceramics,

needlework, woodworking, performing in dramatic productions, and making music. Gardening can be an artistic endeavor. Some of these activities may be the expansion of hobbies nursed through the years. Many older people have discovered within themselves a capacity for art that they did not know they possessed and are finding joy in painting or writing poetry or their memoirs. In the Western world we tend to think of art as a virtuoso activity to be performed only by the gifted for the benefit of sophisticated appreciators and to be preserved in museums. In other cultures everyone is expected to be artistic, and art is considered to be something to do, to be enjoyed, and to be used up.

A student

A fifth avenue for significant activity lies in the search for enlightenment through study, contemplation, meditation, and thought. This might involve reading and research in selected areas or going back to school. Elder Hostel programs at hundreds of colleges provide two-week programs for older people. Many universities now have special courses for older people. Most of them admit older people to degree programs, so that people in their 70s and 80s are working toward degrees.

This might include setting aside time for meditation. The tradition of contemplation and a life of prayer has almost been lost in Western Christendom except in certain contemplative orders within the Roman Catholic Church. Journals and poetry may become vehicles for reflection on life.

A sage

One may also become a teacher or a mentor, guiding others to the state of enlightenment. By virtue of having lived through historical episodes, older people are in a position to be expert witnesses to the meaning of past events. They can serve as the link between generations. Oral histories and memoirs are increasingly prized. But it ought to be emphasized here that before one becomes a teacher who can be trusted, one must have sought and secured enlightenment. Living a long time in itself does not confer wisdom; wisdom has to be sought out. But each of us has a story to tell and a song to sing, and through the telling and the singing we can create a better world.

We can become an encourager and supporter of others as well as a sharer of insight and information. This requires us to be good listeners, to express interest in others, to be fully present to others, and to communicate a loving concern. To hear another is to give them a gift.

If nothing else, we can demonstrate to others who follow how to grow old and how to die with the dignity befitting a human being. We can try to be a model that others will find helpful on their pilgrimage.

One who waits

Finally, we may find ourselves in a situation in which time can only be used in waiting. There is a time when the seed is planted and we can do nothing until it germinates and sprouts and puts forth its stalk. There is a time when the hunter in his blind can only wait for his quarry to come by or when the fisherman can only wait for the fish to bite. There may be a time when we have done all we can and the rest is out of our hands and in the hands of God. This may be the time to sit and let time go by, a time to rest quietly in bed waiting for new doors to open.

A few years back I called on a former teacher and friend of many years. In her 90s she had grown feeble, unable to do anything for herself. Her mind was clear, but she was confined to her bed in a nursing home. When she knew I was coming to visit her, she asked the nurses to dress her in her best dress and to comb her hair. Unable to lift her head, stretched out on her bed with a colorful afghan over her feet and knees, she received me graciously and greeted me warmly. She asked for news of our common acquaintances. She expressed interest in what I was doing. She sent greetings to members of my family. It was about that time she had stopped eating, I learned later. Her younger sister reported that her only complaint was that it was taking so long to die. But while she waited, she was living out her vocation of *being*.

I also have seen persons for whom I have cared deeply, because of a series of strokes, or a condition such as Alzheimer's disease, deteriorate in their last days into completely dependent, incontinent, unknowing husks of persons, often agitated and seemingly in distress. It is heartrending to see them. Sometimes their existence stretches into months and years. We can only hope that they too are serving by waiting and that as they have passed into that limbo they have been able to go trusting in the leading of the Holy Spirit.

The Call to Glory

A man was walking in the park one day and began conversing with another, who suggested they walk together. In the course of the conversation it turned out that the stranger was in reality the devil.

Realizing that the devil had once been an angel and had occupied a seat next to the throne of God, the man was curious. "Do you miss being in heaven?" he asked the devil.

"Well, yes," the devil admitted. "There are some things I miss very much."

The man persisted, "What do you miss the most?"

The devil thought a long time and then pensively he replied,

"I believe that more than anything else I miss the sound of the trumpets in the morning."

Those who serve God in response to his calling can wake up every morning to the sound of trumpets calling them to glory.

CHAPTER SIX

Inherit the Kingdom

From time immemorial human beings have lived in dread of disease, of enmity with others, and of death. We know that as we grow older, our lives are in greater jeopardy, and we run increased risk of being laid low by sickness, of being forsaken, rejected, or neglected by others, and of dying. It is not surprising that we live much of our lives worrying about what might happen. When we do become sufferers, it is not surprising if we become depressed, more fearful, and even despairing.

How can we live a life free from fear? How can we find meaning and joy in the midst of pain and disability? How can we face the prospect of dying with hope and courage?

Sometimes the question is framed in terms of how we can have peace of mind. Sometimes it is put in terms of how we can get the power to endure. Sometimes it is phrased as the search for a satisfying life. Gerontologists sometimes speak of it not only in terms of life satisfaction, but also in terms of a successful old age. In more popular usage it is referred to as the "good life." The Interfaith Coalition on Aging, an ecumenical organization of religious leaders in the field of aging, came up with the term *spiritual well-being* as a rather neutral term for the discussion of the role of religion.

Are these things available to us? And if they are, what do we need to do to obtain them?

Many voices give different and conflicting answers to these questions. Some say the good life is one filled with material things: landed estates, luxurious homes, big cars, fine clothes, and unlimited money. Some say the good life is one of high living with gourmet food, fine wine, sexual conquest, world travel, and excitement. Some say peace of mind is found in money, power, or high social status.

With increasing age these things ring more and more hollow, even when they are frantically pursued.

I believe the answers to these questions are to be found within the Christian teachings about salvation, the kingdom of God, and life eternal—in faith in Jesus Christ, through whom and with whom we are resurrected to a new life. Many of the material things are good in their proper place. But in the Sermon on the Mount Jesus taught:

> So do not worry, saying, "What shall we eat?" or "What shall we drink?" or "What shall we wear?" For the pagans run after all these things, and your heavenly Father knows that you need them. But seek first his kingdom and his righteousness, and all these things will be given to you as well (Matt. 6:31-33).

The Biblical Concept

All three synoptic Gospels recount the story of the man who came to Jesus and asked, "What shall I do to inherit eternal life?" Luke records that the question was asked on two different occasions. Eternal life, contrasted with death, is also a key concept in John's gospel.

Eternal life is the life of the spirit as contrasted with that of the flesh. It is a special quality or outlook that informs a person's whole life and permeates his concrete daily existence. One who possesses this life is no longer afraid of death, no longer lives burdened with guilt, no longer despairs when caught in the toils of illness. The new life is one of power to overcome sin as well as death.[1]

Eternal life is God's gift, an inheritance given to those who will receive it. It is a life lived in accordance with God's will, a life of righteousness, the life which Jesus lived, a life marked by the commitment to love God with all our being and our neighbor as ourselves.

The apostle Paul wrote:

> And this is my prayer: that your love may abound more and more in knowledge and depth of insight, so that you may be able to discern what is best and may be pure and blameless until the day of Christ, filled with the fruit of righteousness that comes through Jesus Christ—to the glory and praise of God (Phil. 1:9-11).

A number of words in the Bible revolve around this concept of life eternal, life in abundance. Among them is *salvation*, sometimes translated "deliverance." As Alan Richardson has put it:

> The Bible is concerned with the fact that God actually has in concrete historical fact saved his people from destruction; and it proclaims that the historical salvation this attested is but the foreshadowing or "type" of the salvation that is to come.[2]

So as I live into my 70s I begin with the reflection that I have survived when many of my contemporaries did not. During my lifetime I narrowly escaped death from accidents. I have recovered from illnesses. I have been forgiven for things I have done wrong.

In the islands of the Aegean Sea, among the whitewashed houses, are many little one-room, white, blue-domed chapels. They contain a simple altar and room enough for a dozen persons. These are monuments or thank offerings built by persons who have been rescued from illness or death on the sea. They are places where the family may gather on occasions to express gratitude for being saved.

The consequence of having been saved is a state of peace or *shalom*—a sense of wholeness, whether of health, prosperity, security, or spiritual completeness, without particular distinction between them. It is a condition in which justice and righteousness prevail. It is a time when borders are secure, order is preserved, justice reigns, good crops ensure prosperity, and the population is freed from pestilence. At this time those of us who live in the United States can be thankful that regardless of whatever other problems we may have, we are not being devastated by war.

Salvation is both present and future, both social and individual. Salvation consists of historical events in which the whole nation is delivered from enemies, from slavery, from destruction, from a lack of identity. Salvation consists also of personal experiences of deliverance from sickness, poverty, and untimely death. The people can point to events on which present existence and well-being depend. Each individual shares in that, although we may not all benefit equally.

The Hebrew prophets saw life and the community whole. For them the abundant life depended not only on the gracious acts of God but also on justice being performed by the people according to God's commandments. In their analysis the abundant life depended on a right relation between persons and their obedience to Yahweh. So Amos predicted the destruction of the nation because its people sold the righteous for silver and trampled on the heads of the poor and the afflicted. Micah pointed out that all the Lord required of his people was to do justice, to love kindness, and to walk humbly with him. If they failed to do this, they would eat but not be satisfied. So the abundant life depends on obedience to the law of God, on behavior and relationships consonant with our nature as beings created in the image of God. Professor Walter Brueggemann of Eden Theological Seminary once remarked that Yahweh differed from all the other gods of the ancient near East because he was more interested in politics than in religion. Politics is the process of doing justice.

The synoptic Gospels also speak of the abundant life in terms of entering into the kingdom of God, of putting oneself under the rule of the Holy One. The apostle Paul writes of the new life that is given as we enter into Christ and become a new creation. Paul also speaks of the resurrection and of living in Christ, as John does. The resurrection occurs in the present when one passes from the death of a sinful existence into life with God (enters the kingdom). Resurrection is not a matter of duration but of a quality of being. It has taken place for those who believe, but it is not completed. Paul notes that he has not yet been perfected but that he presses on for the prize of his calling, which he understands as victory over death.

So the abundant life is the opposite of being "lost." In a lecture Paul Tillich once noted that each great historical era had a different way of experiencing lostness. For the era of the early Christian movement, lostness was the fear of death and the terror of entering into a shadowy world of nothingness. For the Middle Ages and through the Reformation, it was a concern about sin and of being plunged into everlasting punishment. In the modern era, Tillich believed that lostness was experienced mainly by a sense of meaninglessness, emptiness, ennui, and boredom. Probably each of these three ways is still experienced by different persons today.

Life Satisfaction

From a secular point of view, social gerontologists have attempted to measure "life satisfaction," which is an individual's subjective judgment about his or her own condition. Most such surveys reveal that the factors most closely associated with life satisfaction in the later years are good health, economic security, and a spouse or companion of similar physical well-being. One such survey discovered that there is no correlation between "religion" and "life satisfaction." Of those surveyed, 72% believed that religious beliefs were very important, and another 16% thought they were important. More than half attended a religious service at least once a week, 93% believed that God responded to prayer, 89% reported that religion was a help in time of stress and unhappiness. Religion was a help in tolerating frustration but did not provide satisfaction by itself.

This same study classified the respondents as 27% enjoyers, 20% casualties, and 53% survivors. Age itself was not related to their ability to cope. Doubtless we can say that only the 27% believed they were having life abundantly.

To be satisfied is to be filled up, to be sated. It is to have our basic needs met. It cannot be a steady state, for satisfaction can never be permanent. Soon after we have eaten our fill, we get hungry again. This gives point and piquancy to the process of securing, preparing, and eating food. Much of the pleasure lies in the process. But satisfaction also depends on some security about being able to complete the process, not only in the present but in the future as well. So we pray daily for food sufficient for the day: "Give us this day our daily bread." We trust there will be food enough for the morrow. When that hope fails, we are filled with anxiety.

To have life abundantly is to be assured of a place at the Lord's table, and to be in good relations with the Host. To be lost is to be alienated from the Giver and Provider of life and to be cut off from access to that which sustains life. It is to be excluded from the common table, no longer numbered among the fellowship.

Life satisfaction must also be correlated with the ability to distinguish between *needs* and *wants*. *Needs* are those things essential to the sustaining and fulfilling of our being as persons. Abraham Maslow posited a hierarchy of needs in which the lowest level of need had to be satisfied before the higher levels could be dealt with, although in reality that seems to be an oversimplification.[4]

The most basic of all needs are the *survival needs*, usually thought of as the physiological needs for food, shelter, water, fresh air, exercise, and rest. Next come the *sociological needs* of belonging and having a secure status in a group, for without membership in a supportive group we could not survive. The next level includes what might be called the *self needs* or psychological needs of being valued, stroked, and cared for. This is the need for intimacy and confirmation. The final and highest level is the *need for self-realization* or the need to become what we are potentially capable of being.

Wants are what we have come to believe meet our needs, whether in fact they do or not, learned from experience or taught to us by others. Wants are highly susceptible to manipulation and to exploitation by others who have a "bill of goods" to sell us for their profit, regardless of our good. Wants are deceptive. Some things that bring immediate diminution of the sense of need do not meet that need. Wants that do not satisfy are insatiable. Inordinate desire, the classical definition of lust, is not organic, but psychic. What is desired may not be needed, but advertising exists to keep us constantly discontented as well as to tell us what is available.

The struggle between Yahweh and the other gods was an attempt to distinguish between needs and wants and to find the

values that truly satisfy. It was a struggle between the partial
and the whole. It was a struggle to find out what the Creator
was truly like and really intended humankind to be. Isaiah
expressed a theme common to all the prophets:

> Come, all you who are thirsty, come to the waters;
> and you who have no money, come, buy and eat! . . .
> Why spend money on what is not bread,
> and your labor on what does not satisfy? (Isa. 55:1-2).

If one measure of the life abundant is life satisfaction, and
if life satisfaction is tied to economic security, what can we
say about that 20% among us who live near or below the
poverty level? We know that one-fourth of all women 65 and
over who live alone live in poverty. We know that half of
minority women 65 and over who live alone live in poverty.
This suggests that they are denied access to material needs and
have less opportunity to meet their social, personal, and spiritual needs.

Certainly those of us who are more fortunate can join forces
with them to develop ways of ensuring a more equitable distribution of the world's goods and of seeking to eradicate poverty so that the abundant life is made available to all persons.
Surely this is the missionary imperative and the point of Maslow's arrangement of needs in a hierarchy. In spreading the
gospel we deal with the whole persons and all their needs.

But even among those who live in poverty and struggle daily
to find enough to eat and ways to keep warm in winter, to say
nothing of securing adequate health care, we find those who
maintain faith in the midst of the struggle. Courage, gallantry,
humor, and love are found among the poor as well as among
the rich. Many who are poor have coped by putting their wants
for material things in abeyance and reducing life to the bare
physical necessities, while finding ways to meet social, personal, and spiritual needs.

We do not save ourselves. We can only grasp the life pre-server that is thrown to us. Those who are lost wait for others to help them.

Successful Aging

A lso from the secular point of view, social gerontologists have been intrigued with the concept of "successful aging." What is an ideal "old age"—from the point of view of either the individual or society? From the individual point of view it is life satisfaction, a subjective opinion.

From the standpoint of society a successful later maturity is one in which the person embodies the characteristics and values that society believes are best. Beyond that, society considers a successful later maturity to be one in which the person over his or her lifetime has given as much or more to society than he or she has taken out of it. A successful later maturity is one in which a person has been able to minimize the friction and irritation associated with being a working member of the society.

Sometimes, as we become older, we outgrow our fear of social sanctions. Because we have nothing to lose, we may become more honest, more outspoken, more assertive, and more colorful—which is laudable. But there is a danger that we may become preoccupied with self and insensitive to the needs and feelings of others, becoming tyrannical, boring, rude, or even offensive.

Health and the Abundant Life

I n later maturity health, more than anything else, is highly correlated with satisfaction. Health may be among the things we Americans value most highly, judging by the amount of time, attention, and money spent on it. What portion of the gross national product should we devote to health care? What is the most cost-effective system of health maintenance? When do physician, hospital, and health-care personnel charges become too high? Is health care to be available to all, or is it to be rationed on the basis of who can afford it?

The term *health* comes from a root word from which we also derive "whole" and "holy." The healthy life is one in which there is unity within the self, between the self and others, and between the self and the environment. The absence of health is characterized by brokenness, conflict, disintegration, disunity, and hostility—in short, by an inability to function or to relate and thus to satisfy basic needs. Physical well-being, mental health, and spiritual well-being are of one piece.

Health is always finite, contingent, and relative. Only God is one. To be healthy is to be the best we can be. Health is relative to our goals, values, intentions, and expectations. It is relative to the perceived stability and predictability of the environment.

Health is a process of healing, of becoming whole, a continuous process of adjusting and coping. It is a direction. Health may be restored by learning more effective coping strategies, by finding a more salubrious environment, or by finding additional supports. Health may be enhanced by a change of lifestyle, by using material means (medicines) to overcome disease, by cleaning up our environment to reduce toxins and hazards, and by genetic manipulation (as yet only a small possibility).

The popular notion of healing focuses on cure. So people may turn to religion to do what medicine cannot do, that is, bring about miraculous and instantaneous healing—with images of eyeglasses, hearing aids, and crutches thrown aside, the deaf suddenly hearing, the blind seeing, and the arthritic moving freely without pain. In this view health is defined as the absence of symptoms or the absence of pain.

We are now coming to understand that once under way the chronic, degenerative types of disease tend to be irreversible and are not subject to cure, although they may be retarded. However, many of them can be prevented or postponed. So the emphasis in health care is shifting from the cure of disease brought on by abuse, neglect, and destructive life-styles to the prevention of these diseases by teaching persons how to avoid destructive and high-risk activities and by reducing occupational and environmental hazards.

If health is the major factor in life satisfaction, is the abundant life then not available to the 15% to 20% of us who endure severe physical limitations? Or what about those among us who live with so-called terminal illnesses from which they know they are dying? Perhaps an answer is given us by Tish Sommers, founder of the Older Women's League. After a divorce at the age of 57 she discovered that she, like many other women, was left stranded without health insurance and the possibility of only minimum Social Security after retirement. So she devoted more than a decade to the organization of women to secure more equitable treatment from social institutions set up to support persons in later maturity. In an interview at age 69 she spoke of the cancer with which she was struggling while carrying on her organizational work. "I have to decide how much time I will be a cancer patient, and how much time I am an organizer. A year and a half ago, I tried to strike a balance, to limit my activities and be a good cancer patient. But now I've pretty much decided that work comes first. I go to a cancer support group, but the cancer is now in my bones. I want to keep working to get as much done as possible." Her motto remains: "Don't agonize—organize."

Obviously, Tish Sommers lived to the fullest within the gradually decreasing limits left to her. But what about those who are only a shell of themselves because of brain damage? When memory or consciousness has receded to almost nothing, the process of dying is nearly complete. For such the question is no longer moot.

None of us can be completely whole until all of us are healed and made well. But the abundant life is a process and a direction. It is learning to make the best of each situation with courage, humor, and faith. Like the abundant life, health is a present reality and an ultimate goal. When accepted in faith as part of the life process, death is seen as the final healing, in which a person becomes one with the Creator.

Our needs include far more than survival. The parable of the feeding of the 5000 may instruct us. Those who were with Jesus pooled what they had and made the best of it. To their amazement all were fed, with some food left over. For those of us experiencing various kinds of disabilities, health may be the effective marshaling of the capacity we have in the service of our calling.

All of us all of our lives have had to live within limitations. If, as we age, we face diminishing capabilities, we may need to redefine our expectancies and our priorities to make the best use of the freedom left to us. In childhood we lived with weakness and dependence. In our later years we may need to accept both weakness and more dependence than we had grown accustomed to.

Health and the Kingdom of God

To conclude this exploration of the concepts of the good life, the terms *abundant life, health, salvation,* and *the kingdom of God* or *the kingdom of heaven* all point to that ideal condition for which we all long. This is a state in which our needs are fully met and our lives are in harmony with all that is. Since this is an ideal state of perfection or maturity, none of us has attained it completely, but we know it in part. We have here a foretaste. We occasionally reap the first fruits of that harvest that is to be enjoyed in the future. The term *the kingdom of God* implies this will all obtain when all lives are lived in harmony with God's nature and all things are subject to God's will for them.

So our pursuit of the abundant life requires that we discover God's will and commit ourselves to live in accord with it. We can enjoy the kingdom now, but we look for completeness in the future. The abundant life is therefore one of pilgrimage and quest. It is to be measured not by length of time we live but by the way we live. It is not free from hunger and pain. These are incidental and incentives for us on the way.

Our image of this ideal state or "good life" or understanding of the nature of God is flawed by our ignorance and by our sinfulness. So we are presented with inadequate, partial, even conflicting images. The best we can do is to look to those persons who have most fully embodied and demonstrated life in the kingdom. As Christians we look to Jesus as the Christ, the embodiment and revelation of God's being and purpose. But not all see in this light. Not all accept the teachings he lived out. None of us is able to follow as closely as we might want.

Jesus did not live to be an old man. He did not die peacefully in his sleep at the end of his allotted span. We can only imagine what his life and ministry would have been if it had not been cut short. We only know that the central thrust of his life was to do the will of his Father who sent him, to love God and to love all humankind. We then have to decide which image of the good life among the many put before us we will choose to pursue. Our lives will be the testing ground to prove which image and which way is most likely to make us heirs of life abundant.

The life abundant will be attainable for all only in the context of a community that supports healthful living and that in itself is striving to be holy. Leo Simmons, a cultural anthropologist who made a comparative study of aging in various societies, pointed out that the environment must make a long life *possible.*[5] Society must then make old age *worth living.* The fact that we are enabling persons to live out their life span is a magnificent achievement and a great gift to this generation. But our achievement is now challenging us to rethink the meaning of the life abundant. It raises again the question of why we should want to live a long time. It makes us concerned to discover what is required of us if we are to inherit the kingdom that has been promised.

Conditions for Becoming Heirs of Life Eternal

Various students of the aging process and observers of the human scene have reflected upon what we must do if we are to have a satisfying later maturity. While folk wisdom reminds us that luck plays some part in providing us with at least the ingredients and perhaps the possibilities for the "good life," most observers agree that we have responsibility for what we become. We must take charge of our own lives. For each of us our life is a work of art in which we use the materials given us to create what we can rather than to allow ourselves to be manipulated by circumstance.

Developmental Decisions

Erik Erikson, who has become one of the major theoreticians of human development, now in his 80s, believes that at each stage of life we are confronted with the need to work through certain transitions and arrive at certain kinds of life decisions.[6] While focusing mainly on childhood and adolescence, he sees the task of *early adulthood* to be that of learning to establish intimate relationships and of committing oneself to them, lest we become increasingly isolated and alone. The task of the *middle years* of adulthood is to learn to become what he calls a "generative person," one who assumes responsibility for creating and nurturing, lest we stagnate, neither developing nor contributing to society. In the *later years* he sees the major development task as that of developing what he calls integrity, putting life together, seeing it whole, accepting it as appropriate and good, lest we yield to despair. While each of these tasks, and others such as establishing identity, tends to keep coming up at every stage, certain decisions are more central than others at particular periods of life.

Robert Peck, another sociologist, tried to break these concepts down into more specific developmental decisions.[7] In the middle adult years he sees four major kinds of decisions confronting us.

1. We must move from valuing physical power to valuing wisdom. Thus, focus on athletic prowess and pride in physical strength must be replaced by the concern to see things in perspective, to make effective choices among alternatives, and to avoid being trapped by cliches and stereotypes.

2. We must move from what he calls *sexualizing* to *socializing:* in other words, we must redefine both men and women as individuals and as companions, colleagues, and friends rather than as sexual objects. We must come to value the capacity for loving more than sexual potency or attractiveness and to be responsible for others rather than using others for our own pleasure.

3. We need to develop an increasing capacity both to extend and then to shift our emotional investment in others. We need

to learn how to develop and to sustain many "temporary affective relationships," to use other terms. We need to learn how to reach out to others, to take the risk of getting close to others, and then be able to cope with separation as it comes. This is important at this stage, because it is from this point on that we begin with increasing frequency to lose those who are significant to us.

4. We need to become increasingly flexible in our judgments and opinions, more tolerant of differences, increasingly able to entertain new ideas and to adapt to changing conditions. He would see all four of these things as going into what Erikson has called generativity and avoiding stagnation. Perhaps this is one way of saying that to be a "good old man" or "good old woman," we need to begin practicing early.

Dr. Peck then goes on to spell out some of the things that we must do in the later years if we are to live abundantly.

1. He suggests that we need to learn to differentiate between the work role and the self. What are we when we are not teachers, carpenters, mailcarriers, parents, or storekeepers? We need to move from preoccupation with a job to a broader concern for the community as a whole, even though we may see the job as a way to serve the community. This is to say that life is more than work.

2. In the later years we must learn to move from a preoccupation with the body to a transcendence of the body with its aches and pains. We must learn to override disability, chronic disease, and minor discomforts. We must see ourselves as more than how we used to appear. This does not mean that we neglect taking care of our bodies or our personal appearance, but that we are to see ourselves as more than our bodies.

3. In later maturity we must learn to move from a preoccupation with the self to a concern for humankind. This involves a preoccupation with the maintenance of life itself and an acceptance of death as the culmination of life.

A Job Description for Later Maturity

If we can assume that a "successful old age" involves having made the basic decisions described above, we might come up with a job description for growing older and for meeting the conditions whereby we can inherit the life abundant. These suggestions come from many sources.[8]

1. Simplify our lives

One of the things we may have to learn to do as we move into the later years is to simplify our lives by focusing on the essentials and getting rid of the clutter. This may mean having a garage sale or giving away many of the things that become a nuisance to care for. It may mean moving from a large place to a smaller place that is more manageable in terms of income and strength. It may mean resigning from some of the organizations and giving up some of the projects that drain our energy. In our society it is easy to accumulate too many things and to belong to too many groups. It is pathetic to see so many grow old among piles of junk until eventually they are no longer able to summon the energy to get out from under it. Life is more than things; the self is larger than what we possess of material goods.

2. Accept what we are

It is also important to learn to accept what we now are and have been as a unique work of art that we have created out of the materials available to us in the time we have been given. No two of us are alike. No two of us have had the same circumstances or talents to work with. We have done what we could and what we thought we had to do with the materials we had to work with.

As Florida Scott-Maxwell has put it: "You need only claim the events of your life to make yourself yours. When you truly

possess all you have been and done, which may take some
time, you are fierce with reality. When at last age has assembled
you together, will it not be easy to let it all go, lived, balanced,
over?"[9]

The errors we have made, the opportunities we have missed,
the failures we have experienced are as much a part of the
picture of our uniqueness as the successes we have experienced, the good things we have done, and the insights we have
gained.

3. Heal the bitter memories

Perhaps one of the hardest tasks of all is to allow the healing
of the bitter memories accumulated over the years. These include rejections endured, abandonments lived through, trust
betrayed, love turned to hate, dreams disappointed. injustice
suffered, and good intentions misunderstood. These poison the
system, corrode our integrity, and alienate us from others. We
need to get rid of the garbage of unresolved conflict, unfinished
grief work, and leftover anger.

These are behind us. We need to leave them there, forgiving
those who occasioned them, recognizing that we too stand in
need of forgiveness. It helps if we can try to understand why
they did what they did. The parents who failed to provide us
with the home we believe we deserved, the children who did
not meet our expectations, the ones we believed in who proved
to have feet of clay, imperfect even as we are imperfect, doubtless had to deal with pressures that may not have been apparent
to us at that time.

It may help if we can find a confidante or two to whom we
can talk about it, get it out of our system, and then leave it
alone. We need to be effective complainers about what bothers
us but not constant carpers. Continual whining will avail us
little.

4. Be good stewards of our health

Without being preoccupied with our bodies or hypochondriacal about aches and pains, we do have a responsibility to maintain our physical health as well as possible. This means that we practice good physical hygiene. Exercise and activity balanced with sufficient rest, adequate diet, and balanced meals, avoidance of drug abuse or misuse, including that of tobacco and alcoholic beverages—all these pay off in helping us to feel better, to feel better about ourselves, to function more efficiently, and to avoid some of the degenerative processes that disable us.

In order to maintain healthful practices it may be useful to have the support of other persons or to belong to groups that exercise regularly. Loneliness sometimes leads us to overeat. Depression nudges us toward excessive indulgence in drugs or alcoholic beverages. Boredom may cause us to lose our appetite. Lack of interests may cause us to give up on caring about ourselves. Nothing to live for may cause us to focus our attention on our illnesses. So healthful living is a style of life, a set of relationships, and a positive outlook.

5. Reach out to others

Instead of sitting and waiting for others to pay some attention to us, yearning for companionship all the while, we can reach out to others. We can express interest in them—in who they are, what they do, and how they feel. We can listen to them, which in itself is a great gift. We can let them teach us what they know. We can express affection and appreciation. We can invite them to join with us in activities. We will be ready then to share with them. We can treat them as individuals who in themselves are utterly unique and of great value. We can admit interdependence with grace and accept support with gratitude.

This may mean that we will go where we may meet others. Sometimes this will mean joining a group in some activity. It may mean writing letters or using the telephone. In some cases it may mean going to call on someone. If we seek out those who are more alone and lonelier than we are, we may find that easier. We may have to ask persons to come to see us. But when they come, we will let them know how much it means to us.

Most persons like to be touched, and they shrink from touching or being touched only when it seems like an invasion of privacy or an impertinence based on lack of respect or acceptance. As we grow older and lose some of the persons on whom we depended for intimacy and for touching, we may need to find new persons to touch and to let touch us. A warm handshake, a pat on the shoulder, a gentle touch on the arm reassure us of the presence of others. When appropriate and given by persons we value, a warm hug is good for us.

6. Find a reason for being

We do not need to let others lay us on the shelf or overlook the talents we have. We can volunteer to be active in worthwhile enterprises. We need to look for a project or a cause or a person to serve that will ally us with that which is larger than ourselves and which will give social significance to our lives. All we have previously said about work and about calling is applicable here.

There is much in the world that needs doing, or righting, or completing. There are so many persons who need a lift along the way. There are so many things going on that are intriguing to be involved in.

7. See your life in the context of eternity

Our lives are the links between all the generations that have gone before and all the generations that are yet to come. Even beyond that, they are phases in the universe expressing itself.

In one sense the whole universe is bound together as a single living organism.

In *The Immense Journey,* the paleontologist Loren Eisley, whose scientific writing becomes a form of poetry, describes an experience he names "The Slit," [10] On one occasion, while looking for fossils, he happened on a narrow gully eroded into the face of a deep escarpment, a gully that tapered long back until it was a mere slit. He left his horse to graze and worked his way down into the slit, which was about wide enough to admit his body. Far down where the sky above was a narrow band of blue he came face to face with a skull exposed on the surface of the sandstone, the remains of a creature buried long before humankind emerged. He thought first that this animal might have been one of his ancestors. Then he wondered what it was that he was never going to see in the ages ahead, for "we are all potential fossils still carrying within our bodies the crudities of former existences, the marks of a world in which living creatures flow with little more consistency than clouds from age to age." [11] So his mind turns to the immense journey of time.

He continues, "The journey is difficult, immense, at times impossible, yet that will not deter some of us from attempting it. We cannot know all that has happened in the past, or the reason for all of these events, any more than we can with surety discern what lies ahead. We have joined the caravan, you might say, at a certain point; we will travel as far as we can, but we cannot in one lifetime see all that we would like to see or learn all we hunger to know. [12]

Forward into Time

Aging, then, carries us neither up nor down but forward. We anticipate not deterioration but change. The secret of living in the later years so as to inherit the kingdom is no different in a way from what it is in the younger years. Each day comes to us as a gift to do with as we can at whatever age.

The parable of the maidens, five of them foolish and five wise, reminds us to keep alive and alert, to keep our lamps lighted and filled with oil (Matt. 25:1-13). This is followed immediately by the parable of the talents, which reminds us that what we do not use we lose. Then follows the story of the last judgment, in which the sheep are separated from the goats. To the sheep at his right hand the King says, "Come, you who are blessed by my Father; take your inheritance, the kingdom prepared for you since the creation of the world. For I was hungry and you gave me something to eat, I was thirsty and you gave me something to drink, I was a stranger and you invited me in, I needed clothes and you clothed me, I was sick and you looked after me, I was in prison and you came to visit me." In amazement those who had just been given the kingdom wondered when they had done all that. Then the King said, "Whatever you did for one of the least of these brothers of mine, you did for me" (Matt. 25:31-46).

What must we do to inherit life abundant? We have enough of the answer to have a sense of direction. This do, and we shall live.

CHAPTER SEVEN

Live under the Rainbow

Do you remember how you used to look forward to Christmas? how you could hardly wait until you saw what presents were in your stockings and under the tree? how you hoped that you would receive that gift you had been hinting about so broadly? Or do you remember how you waited for the Fourth of July so you could set off firecrackers and join in the celebration with its parades and ice cream and footraces? or how important your birthday was and how you looked forward to it?

Time moved slowly as you counted off the days in eager anticipation. It seemed like the great day would never come and that you could not possibly wait until it arrived. But you could, and it did come. Later on other things and other days became the focus of planning, waiting, and expectation: graduation from school, the first job that paid real money, turning 21 and being able to vote, getting married, the first child, being promoted.

Except for occasional moments of despair, in childhood and youth we lived in hope. We looked ahead. The future beckoned with promises of something far better and more satisfying than the present. The rainbow was a symbol of hope, and we lived believing there was a pot of gold at its foot. If we were stricken with illness, we anticipated recovery. If we were poor, we believed things would get better.

In the middle years our anticipations may have been dulled by too many fulfillments to the point where success became routine and the future was taken for granted. Or else our optimism about the future may have been tempered by a cynicism born of disillusionment and disappointment, so we abandoned hope. But more typically, after we had assimilated the shock of passing 40, our middle years were still buoyed by the hope of dreams still to be fulfilled. There was something to get up for in the morning, something to look forward to, something to anticipate in the future.

But at the same time, in late middle age many of us became aware of and faced the stark limitations that hemmed us in. We may have realized then that there were some doors that probably were closed to us for all time. We had gone as far as we could go in our occupation. We had reached the top of our earning capacity. If we had wanted children and did not have them, it was now too late. Perhaps the children on whom we had pinned such hopes proved to be just ordinary human beings like us. We may have begun to dwell more on opportunities missed and failures experienced than on prospects and possibilities to be anticipated.

Who among us looks forward as eagerly to old age as we did to becoming 21? or to retirement as much as we did to the appointment to our first important job? Who among us finds it hard to wait until we reach 80 or 90 years of age? How often after 50 do we wake up in the morning filled with joyous expectancy that some great and pleasurable event will occur, or that we can look forward to some surprise gift? How often are we aware of a rainbow arching our sky in glorious colors? Wouldn't it be great if we could?

It is not only getting old that dims our hope, but also the period of history through which we are living. In the United States we have passed through an era in which an open frontier always stretched beyond. When the geographical frontier was gone, we still lived with faith in progress and the dream of a tomorrow made better by industrial and technological developments. We believed that our resources were endless, just waiting to be tapped. Visions of a land flowing with milk and honey were so pervasive that persons took incredible risks and endured unbelievable hardships to work in a new place in a new land.

My father's parents packed up their meager belongings and took a ship to America, leaving Germany for the hope of a better life here. They crossed in the steerage, entered through Ellis Island, and made their way by stages across country to the Middle West in search of good land to farm. My father "proved up" a homestead. Both of my parents lived in a sod house 30 miles from the nearest town, scrimping and saving to find some measure of security in hope of a better life for themselves and their children.

My children may not have the same hopeful outlook for making their way up the ladder. In common with the rest of the "Baby Boom Generation" they have encountered fierce competition for jobs, have seen workers displaced by machines, and have lived through more than a decade of inflation that has outrun income.

Now we Americans have become aware of the finiteness of resources and the deleterious effects of constant growth. Many of the improvements we counted on to make our lives better have had the side effects of poisoning our environment and subjecting us to new health hazards. We live aware of the smoke from the Holocaust in Europe, the shadow of the mush-room-shaped clouds over Hiroshima and Nagasaki, and the destruction and defeat in Vietnam. We have become aware of the difficulty of eradicating racism, sexism, and agism, in spite of some progress. We despair of being able to resolve our social conflicts and of fashioning a just and merciful world in which the hand of one is not lifted against another, where terrorism and death squads do not lurk in the shadows. The daily news reports deluge us with tales of catastrophe from all over the globe, until we finally turn our minds off, unable to assimilate or cope with it all.

Many of our children have rejected the values for which we have worked. Some of them have taken the values seriously and revolted against the institutions we thought protected those values. The mood of our time is dark, and hopes are muted. Disillusionment is rife among us. Cynicism has replaced a naive faith in the perfectability of persons and society through education and planning. Hope in inevitable progress has been replaced by pessimism, as we see the roads, the bridges, the streets, and the sewers wearing out, while no one seems willing to pay the taxes to repair them.

Not only is the frontier gone, and not only are our resources becoming depleted, but many of our solutions have led to new conditions worse than the original problems. Recklessly, ig-norantly, greedily, or irresponsibly we manufactured chemicals to kill weeds and insects, only to find that our food is being contaminated. We drilled wells and built irrigation ditches, only to find that the land is slowly becoming alkaline while the water level is going down. We were urged to raise our standard of living with bigger houses, more gadgets, and travel. Then our need for energy threatened to outrun our supply. We cut back on the use of energy and saw prices skyrocket to compensate for lowered use. Now we again have a surplus of energy and must pay for that in higher prices. Inflation continues to erode our purchasing power, and we are told we will have to reduce our standard of living further. This is true especially for those of us who see the constant attack on "entitlements" and efforts to reduce the amount available to us through Social Security and Medicare. We have lost faith in our institutions.

Where can we find the ground and source of hope in the face of the increasing years and the drastic social dislocations? How can we bring joy to our lives? What will enable us to look ahead eagerly to each new day? How can we restore our capacity for surprise and wonder? How can we find occasion to clap our hands and laugh with glee as we did when we were children? Or is all this too much to ask?

Lucille Swartz, as we shall call her, was the widow of a distinguished physician. In the city where she lived she was well-known for her patronage of the arts as a music teacher. She was a friend of many of the city's leading musicians. After her husband's death she moved to a retirement home. There for a decade she contributed leadership to the fine arts programs in the homes, arranging concerts, entertaining visiting performers, overseeing the care of the pianos and organs. Her mind remained sharp and incisive. One morning, in her late 80s, she was found lying on the floor of her apartment, where she had fallen, too weak to get up by herself. She was taken to the infirmary, where she could be cared for.

When I saw her there that afternoon, she grasped my hand and clung to it, visibly agitated, and obviously scared.

"I'm so glad you've come," she said. "I don't know what to do or what is going to become of me now. I have been praying that this would not happen. I had hoped that if I took care of myself and kept active I could avoid this. But now here I am in the hospital, and I may be here the rest of my life. Now I have no future!"

I tried to listen to her fears, to let her know that I understood. I tried to reassure her that she would be taken care of and that she ought not jump too soon to the conclusion that she would never be able to go back to her own apartment. But her statement haunted me.

When I saw her the next day, I said to her, "I have been thinking about what you said about having no future. I wonder what it means for any of us to have a future at any age? What gave you a future when you were younger and in good health?"

She thought for a moment and then said, "I guess it means to live just one day at a time. Maybe it means to have faith that I will be taken care of and that this too will come out all right, no matter what happens. But I am still afraid."

The problem of having a bright future, of having something to look forward to with eager anticipation, is one that faces us frequently in the later years. We know that it is hope that enables us to face that uncertain future in spite of our fears and our trembling.

The Meaning of Hope

Before we look for the ground of our hope and how we can find it, let us define *hope*. *Hope* is the expectation that what we desire will come to pass. It is the anticipation of that which is not yet but is longed for. It is the opposite of dread.

In *The Revolution of Hope: Toward a Humanized Technology* the psychologist Erich Fromm reminds us that we need to distinguish between conscious and unconscious hope, for there are persons who suppress their feeling of hopelessness.[1] Those who have lost hope tend to reduce their demands of life and settle for what they can get. The response of many of us who are older to a question of what we need or want is "Nothing." We tend to harden our hearts against all feeling as a defense against despair. Boredom, inability to relate to other persons, disinterest, and lack of capacity to plan ahead are associated with the loss of hope. We may even give way to violent or destructive behavior if we have no hope.

In their study of *Four Stages of Life* Marjorie Lowenthal and her colleagues discovered that happiness in old age is highly correlated with a future orientation. The longer the extension of this orientation into the future, the more hopeful persons were, the happier they were.[2] It is only when older people are unhappy and without hope that they tend to dwell on the past, remembering it as the time of happiness and fulfillment. Contrary to conventional wisdom, older persons are not the ones who dwell on the past. This preoccupation peaks in middle age.

The Ground of Hope

Some years ago, as I was first gathering notes for this reflection on hope, I found myself in the hospital for an operation on an enlarged prostate. The surgeon warned me that there was a high probability the enlargement would prove to be cancerous. I believe he said the chances were 80 percent. I recall that I brushed off the perception of the 80 percent and girded myself with the hope that it would be benign, betting on the 20 percent.

After the operation I had to wait three days for the laboratory report on the biopsy. During that time I continued to hope that the report would be negative. But secretly I must have sensed that it would be positive. I found that although I could feel no emotion, I was holding myself so tensely that I had severe headaches and pains throughout my shoulders. I had repressed my hopelessness.

Then the surgeon came in with the report that I did indeed have cancer and would need further surgery to be followed by a course of radiation therapy. It took a while to fully assimilate this dreaded news. I called my wife. When she came in, tears began to flow as I told her. Then I burst into sobs. I cried because my hope of evading this disease was shattered. I cried because this seemed to be a sign of lost youth. I cried because this made me think that I had lived out most of my life and that now I walked close to the precipice and could look into the abyss. I cried too because I was scared. I dreaded the thought of more surgery and the days of radiation and of the need to cancel appointments for several months ahead, laying aside plans already set to make some trips to speak and to consult.

But my tears and my sobs were signs that I had accepted the reality of my situation and had begun to shoulder the burden to be carried. As I cried, the tightness between my shoulders relaxed and my headache eased off. I had allowed myself to feel my fear and a little of my anger. Whatever hope I could muster now could be realistic rather than fanciful. I was comforted too by the fact that my wife cried with me. I was not alone in the face of the enemy.

I accepted the surgeon's statement that the prognosis would be excellent and that the surgery would be tolerable and successful. I accepted his assurance that the radiation therapy would control the cancer and in all probability would yield complete remission. I now realized my life was in the hands of God. The powers of life and healing flowed through me. Hope nerved me for the surgery.

The morning I went back into surgery my pastor, Alton Pope, came to see me. My wife was there, as was Dr. Robert Carrigan, a friend of many years' standing, and the wife of the other patient who shared my semiprivate room. The pastor said he would like to lift up in prayer what we had been talking about. He invited the others in the room to participate. The wife of my fellow patient reached out to take the pastor's hand,

and so we all joined hands in a circle as the pastor put into words for all of us our gratitude for God's mercy up to that day. He voiced our trust in God's restorative powers and our hope for healing. This was a deeply moving and supportive experience.

In 1976 Dr. Robert L. Carrigan, professor of pastoral care at Saint Paul School of Theology in Kansas City, published a paper on hope. In this paper he noted,

> The hoping person exists, then, within a wider reality that transcends him or herself. The lone person can only wish, for hope cannot be experienced alone, apart from the hoping community. The community is the sustainer and vehicle of hope, and humankind always hopes *with,* whereas isolation contributes to hopelessness.[3]

Dr. Carrigan saw hoping as a shared experience born out of a realistically tragic sense of life. In this experience "together we can catch a glimpse of some new ground and new possibilities within the old realities." He went on to say,

> In hoping, because of its relational character, we participate in what we hope for, yet we know ourselves as part of a larger reality that transcends our private worlds.[4]

I found that to be true for me when I saw death standing outside the door and did not know if this was my time to take death's hand.

Dr. Carrigan planned to take a sabbatical leave from teaching early in 1984 to do more research and to write a book on hope. But in the summer of 1983 he became seriously ill of a combination of immune deficiency and leukemia. After five months of struggle he succumbed to the disease at the age of 56. I stood by his bedside with his family as his blood pressure dropped to zero and the pulse meter straightened out. During all those long days of illness he lived hopefully, even after he realized that probably he would never recover. All of us, his family and his many friends, were privileged to share in his ebbing life.

In my own case, my surgery was successful and attended with only minor inconvenience and a modicum of pain, the memory of which is softened by time. The pathologist reported that an examination of the lymph nodes revealed that the cancer had not spread. This meant that the malignancy was contained and could be readily treated by radiation. Hope was fortified by faith in the demonstrated skill of the surgeon, the competency of the pathologist and the radiation therapist, and the healing power of the human body. Hope was also engendered by the knowledge that in a high percentage of cases treatment had been successful. The love and concern of friends and family as well as the compassionate care of the nursing staff gave me courage and reason for living. Hope fortified me through the tedium of two months of daily radiation therapy. Hope kept me going through the periods of depression fluctuating with anger following treatment.

"What," asked my radiation technician, "is the difference between hope and faith?" Quite simply, I responded, faith was the readiness to trust myself completely into the hands of the medical team, to allow them to put me to sleep with the anesthetic, to perform surgery, and to expose me to radiation. Faith was confidence in their competency and their compassion. Hope was the belief and the expectation that all this would assist in restoring health.

After treatment and after five years with no return of the problem, a bone scan indicates that the cancer may again be active. So I am now taking hormones with the hope of arresting the disease. My future is still uncertain, as it has always been and always will be. However, hope allows me to make plans and take on projects that stretch several years ahead. Hope lets me rejoice in each day as it comes. It lets me anticipate the days yet to come.

Past experience with recovery from illness and the knowledge that others have recovered from similar illnesses were important ingredients in my hopefulness. Children who have limited experience must derive their hope almost entirely from faith in the veracity of their parents or significant others. Those of us who have lived through many vicissitudes can draw upon our own experience to be able to transcend the difficulty of the moment.

John Macquarrie supports this. He writes:

> If there were no past experiences, either our own or reliably reported, of apparently "hopeless" situations which had been resolved by the interruption of the new and the hopeful, and if there was no possibility of hope in our present experience, then we could have no hope for the future. The human self has always past, present and future dimensions, and needs all three to be genuinely a self. If a free undetermined space in the future is needed for selfhood and identity, so is a history and a tradition from the past.[5]

Two conditions present the gravest challenge to hope. One is the condition of satiety, in which everything is available, nothing is lacking, nothing must be deferred. Because need is absent and challenge is lacking, boredom and ennui set in. There is nothing to look forward to. One forgets to be grateful. Perhaps this was the situation of the rich young ruler who came to Jesus to ask what he could do to secure eternal life. After learning that he had kept the commandments—at least to the letter—Jesus told him to sell all he had, give it to the poor, and follow him. As it was, he had nothing to look forward to and hardly dared to hope for that which wealth could not provide.

The other challenge to hope comes from extreme deprivation and suffering. It is precisely in those so-called hopeless situations that Christian hope becomes the resource enabling persons to find meaning and purpose in life. The concentration camps of World War II, the "boat people" who stake their lives on a wild and desperate gamble that they can make it to a safe harbor and find a welcome, the refugee camps for those fleeing from persecution for their political beliefs or from the devastation of war—these are paradigms of the seemingly hopeless situation in our time. Hope finally is what we live by when planning is no longer possible and when there is nothing we can do that will get us out. This is the hope that sustains us when we have been told we have a terminal illness.

Hoping Against Hope

The psychology of the concentration camp has been most vividly and precisely described by Viktor Frankl, the Viennese psychiatrist who lost his wife, his parents, and his brothers and sisters in the gas chambers of Buchenwald and Dachau, and in which he spent several years of his own life, often on the verge of death.[6]

He indicates that there are three phases of an inmate's existence in the camp.

The first period follows his admission. This period is characterized by shock, by a clinging to straws, by a cherishing of the delusion of a reprieve. Next the prisoner strikes out from his whole life the former existence as an illusion. This then is followed by the cultivation of a macabre sense of humor, a morbid curiosity about what is going to happen next, and surprise that so much can be endured and withstood.

The second phase comes when the prisoner is well-entrenched in the camp routines. This period is often characterized by apathy. One builds a shell of insensitivity, a kind of self-anesthetization, as a form of defense against despair. In this phase the entire focus of the self is on survival, often to the point of becoming completely careless about the survival of any of the others. However, it is in this situation, says Dr.

Frankl, that the inner life can deepen and one can grow richer in spiritual freedom. One may become more sensitive to moments of beauty. The minutes become precious. One compares one's lot with that of others who may be worse off. One is grateful for the smallest mercies. Here one can demonstrate self-denying compassion for others, even to the giving of one's own life for their survival.

The third period is that which comes after release and liberation, if one survives the second period. It is a time when one has to put the past behind and go on to a new phase of life, not denying, but not dwelling on, the past, using what has been learned in the past for life in the present.

In the concentration camp it is difficult to hold on to a consciousness of inner value in the face of being treated as a nonentity. There is a tendency for prisoners to suffer from an inferiority complex, for all the symbols and rituals that indicate their status have been taken away, along with their power to choose their own life.

For me the concentration camp is an example of situations many of us find ourselves in. Dr. Frankl's observations about life in the concentration camp square with what I have seen in other situations, although no other situation can match the horror of the death camps founded for the purpose of genocide.

Perhaps the thing many of us dread most is the possibility that we might end our days in a nursing home as a long-care patient. If so, we will be there not by choice but necessity. Once there, as we become powerless, other persons tend to stop taking us seriously and begin to patronize us, if not to abuse us, dropping our titles, the badges of the status we have earned. We find ourselves having to fit our needs and desires into the routines that enable the institution to function at maximum efficiency with minimum bother for the staff. Too often the relationships and care given in such settings become mechanical and impersonal. We become cases rather than persons.

Then comes the temptation to give up hope and to resign ourselves to dying, or else to lash out in anger against the staff and caretakers and dream of escaping or of being liberated.

Dr. Frankl attests that even in such situations one does have a choice of action and can preserve a vestige at least of spiritual freedom, as well as independence of mind. The person one becomes in such a setting is the result of an inner decision. The way one bears suffering and accepts one's fate constitutes an inner achievement. Whereas most of our life we find our meaning in activity and in achievement or in enjoyment, in such situations meaning may have to be found in suffering. Dr. Frankl believes that meaning has to be found in the present and not in hope of escape or liberation. Even though we can foresee the approaching end of an existence that fate has taken out of our hands, we can face the situation, because we know we participate now in life eternal.

Just as faith has not been tested until we have wrestled with doubts, so hope has not been tested until we find ourselves with something like cancer when treatment is futile. For those who know they are terminally ill and for whom death draws near, hope is to be found in the possibility of making good use of the time still available hour by hour, bearing witness to what love can do even then. Hope is to be found also in the expectation that death itself is the last great healer, marking the completion of one phase of being and the beginning of another, the release and liberation from the earthly to the heavenly.

So hope is like a concentric ring of defenses around a fortress. As the outer defenses fall, we retreat to one inner ring and then to another, until we take our last stand within the fort itself. As we do so, we know that even if that falls, in the long run the victory is ours, for as we fight a losing battle, we are helping to win the war, and the kingdom will be ours.

I hope that my disease will be healed. If it cannot be, I hope I may yet live for a time and that life will be good while I am living. When the time has come for me to die, I hope that whatever lies beyond death will be good, because God has planned it.

Jesus Pioneered and Perfected Our Hope

On the cross, Jesus accepted and transcended that which was laid on him in hatred, making it the means for redeeming and transforming the world. He did not seek that end, but neither did he shirk it when there was no other way out. He experienced the loneliness of suffering, even to despairing of God's presence. But at the end he could say to the repentant thief, "Today you will be with me in paradise." Finally, he could pray, "Father, into your hands I commit my Spirit" (Luke 23:43,46).

In the power of his commitment to his calling, Jesus rode out the storm of rejection, persecution, and crucifixion, fulfilling the hope and expectation of Israel for the Messiah. Through this ministry he brought into being a new community, the kingdom of God, the body through which his ministry would be continued and extended. His faith became the faith of those who found new life in this community.

The Christian gospel is a gospel of hope, which was heard most gladly by subjugated, outcast, enslaved, and displaced people. This gospel was that God's rule would be established over all the earth, and there would be a final judgment in which those who believe in Christ would be acquitted and given a renewed and continuing life in the presence of the Lord of life. Those who live by that hope are called to participate with God in those actions by which God is bringing this about. The cross and the resurrection, on which our hope rests, belong together as a single act; to participate in the life of Christ is to live the way of the cross.

In Norman Young's words:

> Our hope is based on the recreative initiative of the Creator
> God, manifest in Jesus Christ, whose power was written off as
> powerlessness. Action that reflects that self-giving love, refus-
> ing to retaliate in kind to aggression and injustice, should no
> longer be relegated only to the area of individualistic piety. It
> is a realistic condition for peace among races, classes, com-
> munities and nations that have fallen apart and threaten to de-
> stroy each other.[7]

The rich and the powerful did not hear this gospel gladly,
because they hoped for a stabilizing of their status and the
establishment of their security through unchallenged domina-
tion. To bring this about they tried persuasion first, but when
persuasion was ineffectual, they used coercive power. Their
concern was not for humankind but for their own kind. But in
spite of all they could do, they too succumbed to death, which
put the meaning of their lives in question.

So while hope means waiting on the action of God to accomplish his purposes, it also requires from us that we participate as much as we are able in God's action—creating as he
creates, loving as he loves, enduring as he endures. What is
hoped for is the reign of God over all the earth, but that reign
begins with each of us acknowledging God's sovereignty and
living by his will.

My wife, Mary Carolyn, had a cousin, David C. Clemans,
who at the age of 24, while with the military in Southeast Asia
in the Second World War, began to suffer symptoms of multiple
sclerosis, not accurately diagnosed for some years. Nevertheless, after the war he completed medical training under the GI
Bill of Rights. He went into practice in a small Oklahoma
town, constantly working with increasing disability, moving
from general practice to anesthesiology, to hospital adminis-
tration—in each case serving with distinction, even from his

wheelchair. Then at age 54 he learned that he had untreatable cancer.

A year before he died, with the encouragement of his pastor, he began to write the history of his battle with disease and to keep a journal for any possible benefit to those who might come after him. Three months before he died he wrote,

> As death approaches I think more and more about the future. I am convinced there is a life after death, and even though I do not know the nature of this life, I feel it will be something wonderful. . . . It is this faith that enables me to continue.[8]

Two months later he resigned from his position as medical director at the hospital. Less than two months after that he was dead. In death as in life he was a witness to the power of hope.

Several years ago I was returning from a sad trip to inter the body of my mother in a grave beside that of my father in another state. She had died at the age of 89 after a long debilitating illness. It was a day made more gloomy by heavy low-hanging clouds and occasional showers of cold rain. My wife, my son and daughter, and my two grandchildren were with me. As we drove homeward in a southeasterly direction, a heavy thunderstorm with lightning and high wind moved across our path in the distance. It looked for a while as if we would be in for heavy weather. But the storm moved so rapidly in front of us that it outran us. Then the late afternoon sun broke through, creating a huge rainbow arching perfectly across the eastern sky, even while lightning played behind it. We were struck by its beauty but at the same time immensely cheered by that ancient symbol of hope, reminding us that life goes on and that in the wake of the storm new life springs forth.

The rainbow is the symbol of hope, because it always appears after a storm. We can wait out the storms when they come, knowing that they always pass and that the sun always shines behind the passing cloud.

George Matheson lost his eyesight at age 18. In spite of his affliction he graduated from the University of Glasgow. At age 26 he became the pastor of a small parish where he served for 18 years and soon became widely known for his preaching and writing. Then he was transferred to a large church of 2000 members in Edinburgh, where he served with distinction for another 13 years. But in spite of this success, his blindness had forced him to give up the life of scholarship to which he had aspired. To make it worse, the girl whom he loved jilted him. Some years later, on the day of his sister's marriage, he was sitting alone in his manse. The magnitude of his loss swept over him again. Then in the midst of his despair, remembering a deeper and more lasting love, he was inspired to pen the lines of a hymn loved by countless worshipers:

> *O Love that wilt not let me go,*
> *I rest my weary soul in thee;*
> *I give thee back the life I owe,*
> *That in thine ocean depths its flow*
> *May richer, fuller be.*

My friend Robert Carrigan saw that hope has to be rooted in our relationships. It is in that relation to the source of love from which there is no separation that our hope ultimately rests.

CHAPTER EIGHT

A Time to Die

Most of the time we think very little about our own death. It is only when we are jolted by the death of someone we know or someone close to us that we are forcefully reminded of our own mortality. Generally we go about our business as if we would live forever. Only occasionally are we made to recollect that after all we will not escape the fate of all other creatures. Perhaps this is to the good. For, after all, it is the business of living that needs our attention. Dying is only incidental to living. Death is another transition to be faced, prepared for, and lived through.

During the time I was administrator of a retirement community where half of the residents were 85 years of age or over, death was a frequent, even a familiar, visitor. Hardly a week went by but some resident died. Some died after long periods of extreme frailty, but most died rather suddenly or after a short illness. The funeral services usually were held in the chapel of the home. Many of the residents came to pay their last respects and to say farewell. For a time old friends the deceased talked about their relationship to them and were keenly aware of a vacancy at the dining table or in the game room, but then their attention turned to other things. Death was seldom longed for or made welcome, but in that setting it did not seem inappropriate. Neither was it a preoccupation.

As we grow older, we do become more interested in the obituary columns of the newspaper, because we so often see there the names of friends or persons we knew or famous contemporaries. As we read these names, we do feel a sense of loss. But if a pastor, visiting the retirement home of which I was the administrator, preached in the chapel on the subject of death, assuming that this was a priority issue with the residents, he was received with polite amusement, indifference, and some scorn for misreading their interests. They wanted to know how to get the most out of the time before them.

In the main, those of us who are older are not the ones who are preoccupied with death. The concern about dying comes earlier, in late middle age, when persons begin to reevaluate their lives and ask themselves what life is all about. By the time we have reached later maturity, most of us have come to terms with our own dying. Under some circumstances we may begin to look forward to it as a release from cares or pain or disability.

In his essay "Aes Triplex" Robert Louis Stevenson commented on this lack of concern about death among the old as well as the young. He noted that after 70, living is like walking forward on increasingly thin ice, but still we press on, and this is the way it should be. It is not that we are in love with life but with living, so that even in old age we continue to make long-range plans and take risks to accomplish them. He suggests that no matter how much longer we have to live, it is never too late to begin a new project. It is in this spirit that the comedian George Burns elicits happy laughter when he announces that he has signed a ten-year contract to play at Caesar's Palace in Las Vegas.

This is the way it ought to be. Our focus should not be on our dying but on living as fully as we can from day to day. However, that focus needs to be balanced by some thought for the future and a sense of responsibility to others, based on the knowledge that we have a limited number of years ahead of us. It is incumbent on us to do some estate planning and to make a will in order to provide for our dependents. We need to direct the disposition of any residual resources according to our values and our wishes. We want to prevent the unnecessary expense and inconvenience to any survivors occasioned by those who die without a will. Also it is incumbent upon us in this day of new medical technologies to give guidance to those who may have to care for us if we become unable to care for ourselves, and to save them the burden of making difficult decisions about how we die and how our remains are to be disposed of after death. Having said all that, it is still true that most of us find it hard to sit down and make these decisions, because death seems so far off and we would rather not think about it anyway.

However, it is this very awareness of our mortality that gives rise to philosophy and religion, that leads us to evaluate how we spend our precious, limited time, that spurs us to use wisely "this brief candle," and makes us exercise caution to fend off an untimely demise, balancing this caution with the concern to live fully even at some risk of death. It is this knowledge that makes us appreciate the gift of each succeeding day and each new season of the year.

Attitudes Toward Death

In our time many of us seem to go to great lengths to deny the possibility of impending death and to conceal or camouflage the reality when it happens. Because so few of us die at home and so often funerals are private affairs, it is possible for most of us to go about our business for years without seeing anyone die or encountering death. So we become persuaded that we will live forever. The sick are taken to hospitals. The decrepit are cared for in nursing homes. We seldom see those who are ill or dying.

Until recently the high rate of infant mortality and the prevalence of early death from infectious or contagious diseases made dying a commonplace phenomenon. Not only did death lurk constantly on the outskirts of each person's journey, but persons died at home. Perhaps the fact that death is now a stranger makes it more fearsome, just as dying in the alien environment of a hospital or nursing home is more frightening.

Not every period of history has feared death as ours seems to. In his book *The Hour of Our Death,* Philippe Aries provides us with a history of funerary practices and attitudes toward death from the late Middle Ages until the present.[1] He identifies five approaches to death that have been prevalent at different times over the last thousand years.

First there was the *tame death* in which the living were present among the dead. The churches were in the midst of graveyards. Mausoleums were constructed in the homes of the wealthy. Death was taken for granted. Only sudden death was feared, because this deprived one of an opportunity to prepare for it. Death was public and communal, governed by familiar rituals. Most persons shared a common and an unmarked grave.

Then there was the *death of the self* period in which there was an individualistic approach to life, and in which one died alone before God to be judged to eternal life or eternal damnation. The soul was thought to be the essential and enduring element of personality. Persons lived in dread of the possibility of burning eternally in hell's fire.

The third period was one in which death was *remote and imminent* at the same time; death was diffused into the whole of life and diluted into melancholy over the brevity of this life. Deathbed conversions were no longer regarded as effective. There tended to be a preoccupation with the violence of nature. Eroticism was often associated with death. There was a fear of being buried alive.

In the fourth period death was *romanticized*. Persons dwelt on descriptions of beautiful deaths. A cult of the dead arose with visits to the cemetery, an attachment to the body, and an insistence that each body should have a suitable coffin and that the grave be marked by a monument.

The final period is the one we seem to be in. In this period death is *invisible*. Death is banished from public notice. Mourning is suppressed or private.

Herman Fifel notes in *New Meanings of Death* that the consciousness of death becomes more acute during periods of social disorganization.[2] These are times when grief becomes deritualized, and community support in bereavement is weak. Certainly ours is a period of transition and disorganization. This may explain why we have privatized death and why we are so confused in our responses to it.

Even so, when we become aware of death, we still have profound and disturbing questions. Why must I die? Is God the designer of a life that must end inevitably in death? Since I will die eventually, how can I prepare myself to die with a dignity commensurate with my stature as a human being? How can I conquer my fear of death? When those I love and depend on die, how can I assimilate their loss without being devastated?

Death in the Judeo-Christian Tradition

In the Old Testament death was recognized as inescapable. In the words of Psalm 90: "The length of our days is seventy years—or eighty, if we have the strength; . . . they quickly pass, and we fly away." We are like the grass of the field or the flower that springs up in the morning and withers at night. Life for most was short. The risks of living were manifold. Old age was a rare gift seen as the special reward for especially righteous living. When a reasonably normal life span was achieved, when one left children to perpetuate the family line, and when the dead were properly buried, death was accepted. There were expected rites of passage, such as the bestowal of a blessing by the dying and the tearing of garments and putting ashes on the head by the bereaved.

But the destructive aspect of death also was recognized. A premature death was thought to be punishment for sin, or the result of the incursion of a hostile power. In an early period there seemed to be the belief that after death one fell into Sheol, which was beyond the realm of Yahweh, ruled by other divinities. But then the prophets saw Yahweh as controlling even Sheol. Since death did not happen without the permission of God, either there had to be a good reason for it to happen, or God had to be over against death.

In the New Testament writings of Paul death is seen both as the wages of sin and the last enemy to be overcome. Paul sees death as overcome through the action of Christ's death and resurrection, so that in Christ all of us may be resurrected. Death's sting is still sin, which results in death-in-life. Through living in Christ and having in us the mind of Christ, we are born again into a spiritual life and transcend the realm of the purely physical. This is eternal life.

Perhaps it is not the fact of our dying so much as our consciousness of our mortality that arouses anxiety. This awareness of our mortality distinguishes us from all other creatures, most of whom are unconcerned about death because they do not know they will die. They have only a drive and an instinct to keep on living until their life has run its course. But it is this same consciousness that can goad us to see our lives in the context of eternity, and that led Paul to exclaim, "Where, O death, is your victory? Where, O death, is your sting?" (1 Cor. 15:55). Not even death can separate us from God's love or God's presence.

Throughout our history attitudes toward death have varied, with considerable ambivalence between horror and fascination. The recognition of mortality and a concern with the end of all things (eschatology) leads us eventually to a concern for mortality, particularly the mortality of God.

As A. Roy Eckhardt puts it,

> The tormented hope of some who today speak from within the Judaic and Christian traditions is not that they will never die but that God must not die: on the other hand, they yearn for God to die their small deaths at their side. Who will win, in the end, Death or God? Faith and love join hope in the testimony that death is sentenced to death.[3]

Our hope is as Isaiah writes:

> He will swallow up death forever. The Sovereign Lord will wipe away the tears from all faces (Isa. 25:8).

This note is repeated in the Book of Revelation.

> Now the dwelling of God is with men, and he will live with them. They will be his people, and God himself will be with them and be their God. He will wipe every tear from their eyes. There will be no more death or mourning or crying or pain, for the old order of things has passed away (Rev. 21:3-4).

Says Will Herberg:

> The whole point of the doctrine of the resurrection is that the life we live now, the life of the body, the life of the empirical existence in society, has some measure of permanent worth in the eyes of God and will not vanish in the transmutation of

things at the "last day." The fulfillment will be a fulfillment of the *whole* man for *all* men who have lived through the years and have entered into history and its making.[4]

The death of the individual is an aspect of the economy of God's creation, but also designed into that creation is the possibility of overcoming the fear of death through faith and the experience of the new birth. There is a time to die. There also is a way to live that leads to life eternal.

Death Is Not a Tragedy

So often after a death occurs persons will say, "What a tragedy!" It is sad when those we love die. It may be catastrophic for one who is left with burdens to bear. It violates our sense of justice when one who is leading an exemplary life, or a life filled with promise, is cut off by untimely accident or killed viciously. But what is tragic is the way life is lived when talent is wasted, when energy is spent in destruction, when promise is unfulfilled, not because of outside forces so much as personal decision. War is tragic because it is the manifestation of hatred and greed and pride.

There is no tragedy in the death that occurs after a full and active life, lived without any noticeable loss of capacity, status, or ability to enjoy life fully. The late Bing Crosby participated in a celebration of his 50th year in show business, in which he demonstrated his continuing professional competence by singing. A few months later, he finished a golf game and dropped on the way to the clubhouse. Others may slow down and then die peacefully in their sleep. Such deaths, while the occasion for grief on the part of those left behind, are generally regarded as good and enviable. "That," we say, "is the way to go."

There is no tragedy in the death of an Arthur Fiedler, who died after a few months of illness, having completed a half century with the Boston Pops Orchestra, universally beloved and admired. He had fulfilled his destiny. But it was not that he had lived long that kept it from being a tragedy, but that he had lived so well in terms of using his talent.

In fact, there is no real tragedy in the death of a young person whose life has been rewarding up to the time of death, although we may regret that such a person did not have more years to contribute to the world. A mother told me of a son who had died in an automobile accident at the age of 20. She described how much he enjoyed life, how excited he was about the opportunities that came his way to express himself through his music, how he had many friends, how thoughtful and loving he was. She said, "I can only be grateful that I had such a son, if only for 20 years. Those 20 years were a joy and he had a good life. All of us are richer for them."

Others, however, are not so fortunate as to die suddenly or to die in full possession of all their powers. Some experience marked deterioration and suffer the ravages of crippling diseases that restrict their freedom and bring them pain. For some the last years are a time of loneliness, emptiness, regret, and a sense of having nothing left to live for. Still others sink into comatose conditions that may go on for a long time, or live a vegetative existence, the cause of great effort and expense of others. To the extent that persons die in neglect and loneliness and dehumanization, the tragedy is that of those around them and not theirs. For those who die slowly over a period of years of some degenerative disease tragedy arises out of inability to transcend it.

An elderly friend of ours died of bone cancer that wasted her slowly over a number of years while undergoing painful surgery and treatment. An ebullient, vigorous woman with a keen sense of humor, she was finally bedfast. A couple of days before she died, when my wife went to see her, she beckoned my wife close to her bed because she could speak only in a whisper and told her a bawdy story. When finished, she chuckled and said, "There, that will brighten up your day!" With that she laid back and closed her eyes. Her death was not tragic, because her life was triumphant.

Dr. James V. Thompson, a mentor of mine, used to say that the only persons who fear to die are those who have never lived. Death is appropriate at the end of the life span and when that span, or the time we have, has been well-lived. Death is tragic when potential is wasted and creativity degenerated into destructiveness of self or others.

When I was a young pastor, I called on an elderly woman in the hospital. As we talked one afternoon, she said, "Well, I have just gotten some rather shaking news. The doctor told me this morning that I have an inoperable cancer. He said it might be six weeks or six months I have left to live."

As we talked, I noticed her composure and said, "You do not seem to be afraid or greatly upset about it."

She replied, "No, I am not afraid of death. In fact I have always been rather curious about things. I think it is going to be a great adventure to find out what it's like on the other side. The only thing that worries me is how I am going to break the news to my family."

She was a strong woman with a deep faith in the future and an openness to what it might hold. She faced death as she had all the other challenges of life, focusing her concern more on those she loved than on herself. But even she must have had her moments of hesitation. Most of us drag our feet as we approach death, and we cling to life.

Reasons for Resisting Dying

Why am I reluctant to die? Like the diver teetering on the edge of the diving board far above the water below, why am I scared to let myself go and drop into the pool below? I remember now that I was scared even before I stepped out on the diving board, even as I considered making the dive.

I do not want to die, because there are things I want to do yet. I do not want to die, because I do not want to be separated from those I love. I am anxious about dying, because it means going off into the dark unknown.

I do not want to think about dying, because I dread the possibility of a long, drawn-out, and helpless old age before I die. As one of my relatives put it in the last year of her life, unable to stand by herself, "It is taking so long." I do not want to be a burden and an expense to those I care about. While I do not want to be a burden, I also fear that I might die among strangers, dependent on persons I do not know.

At the age of 82 Florida Scott-Maxwell wrote,

> My only fear about death is that it will not come soon enough. Life still interests and occupies me. Happily I am not in such discomfort that I wish for death; I love and am loved, but please God I die before I lose my independence.[5]

I do not want to think about dying, because I dread the possibility of long drawn-out discomfort and pain either from disease or the treatment of disease.

What Is a Good Death?

So, recognizing that I must die, how would I want to die? First of all, I would choose a time to die at the end of my life span, when I have had opportunity to savor all the years and to see what I could do with them, when I have completed my projects. This assumes that I could retain my faculties and enjoy life until the end.

Then I would hope that death would come quickly, preferably when I am asleep. But I would want to be prepared for it by having my affairs in reasonably good order. When I was a college student, I was deeply impressed by the way in which my professor of philosophy, Dr. Edward Lewis, faced a terminal illness and planned for his death. His affairs were all arranged for the benefit of his family. He helped to plan the memorial service held for him and the manner of his burial.

I hope that I will not have too much pain when I die, and that is the reason I hope to have it happen quickly. Here I am helped to know that while pain may be experienced during illness or injury, in terminal situations, as in traumatic situations, there seems to be some biological mechanism that anesthetizes us. In any case, it is now possible to control pain fairly well through medication and counseling.

It is out of this concern with a good or easy death (in Greek the word is *euthanasia*) that the hospice movement has come into being in our time. The hospice program is committed to assisting persons to die free from pain and surrounded by friends, not preparing them for death as such, but enabling them to live as fully as possible each day. This concern has given rise also to the "Right to Die" and "Death with Dignity" discussions, which have resulted in new legislation, the formulation of new codes of ethics, and the writing of living wills.

New Decisions Set Before Us

Today, for the first time in history, developments in the field of medicine have equipped physicians and other health-care professionals with a vast array of new drugs and with new surgical tools and techniques.

Life-support machinery and artificial organs have opened possibilities that never existed before. Not only have these developments made possible the saving of life and increased the likelihood that we will live out our life span, but they also have confronted us with decisions we have never had to make before. Like most decisions these are fraught with ambiguity and risk. The widening of the perimeters of freedom has increased the burden of choice.

When an illness is obviously curable or a condition reversible, and when the treatment will both free the patient from pain and enable him or her to function at a relatively high level for considerable time, there is little problem. Although all treatments have a degree of risk, when the risk is small and the prognosis good, we do not hesitate.

But then we have to make a decision about whether or not to use expensive, cumbersome, inconvenient, and often uncomfortable procedures to prolong life for a relatively short time. At what point do we seek, accept, or tolerate aggressive and so-called heroic measures to prolong life? At what point do we refuse treatment and let nature take its course?

At this juncture we may have to decide if we want to live, and if we consider the extra time to be worth the trouble and expense. We may have to weigh the consequences of either course, not only in light of what it means for us individually but what it means for those around us.

Howard Thurman, a distinguished preacher and former dean of the chapel at Boston University, told an annual meeting of the Western Gerontological Society that he had faced such a decision when he had been hospitalized and diagnosed as needing extremely risky surgery. He had to make the decision whether or not to go through with it. His first response was that he needed more time to think about it. He requested that he be left alone for several hours. Then he reported that for the first time in his life he really had to wrestle with the question of whether or not he wanted to live or whether it was time to die.

On still another level we may have to decide whether or not to undergo procedures that might save life and prolong it for a time but which might leave us severely impaired mentally. For example, a brain tumor might be excised so that it no longer threatens life, but mental functioning might be so greatly impaired that we would be little more than a zombie. A similar question arises in regard to resuscitation from a cardiac arrest.

A professor emeritus of Stanford University Medical School, Dr. Louis S. Baer, believes that the danger of brain damage from cardiac arrest is so great after age 65 that he wears a medical alert to instruct caregivers not to attempt resuscitation after two minutes.[6] My wife and I also have given similar instructions and have filed them with our physician as part of our living will.

In his book *Let the Patient Decide,* Dr. Baer goes much further and directs that in case he has to be placed in a nursing home, and if he becomes incompetent to make a decision and is unable to feed himself, he shall not be fed. He wants to receive nursing care but no medical treatment, because he does not want to be kept alive in a comatose or vegetative state.

This raises a still more difficult kind of decision. When a patient becomes incompetent to decide because of being unconscious, the caregiver may be left with the decision of whether or not to refuse or discontinue medical treatment or what kind of treatment to provide—unless the patient has already made such a decision in advance and has left explicit instructions.

Once on a plane between Madison and Chicago, I fell into conversation with an elderly woman who was my seatmate. She told me that her 74-year-old husband had been in a coma for 14 months, able to move only one finger on one hand, completely unresponsive, as a result of a massive cerebral hemorrhage. Every few weeks the catheter had to be changed, and when this was done it often resulted in an infection of the urinary tract, which had to be treated with massive doses of antibiotics. Recently the physician had told the wife that if the penicillin were not given, the patient would soon die. He said that if she said not to give the penicillin, he would not do it. To make the situation more poignant, they had promised each other that should something like this happen, heroic measures would not be used to prolong life. She was in the throes of making that decision. When we parted at the airport, I did not know what her decision would be. What would you have done? Certainly it would have helped if he had made a living will to document his own decision.

In any case these difficult decisions are best made in consultation with the parties involved and in full view of all the known facts. Medical personnel, family, friends, and clergy might help to make the decision.

One of the problems in making such decisions is that those involved often experience great pressure from distant relatives, members of the community, and even the legal system to decide in particular ways. Sometimes the pressures are conflicting. These too have to be taken into consideration but for no more than they are worth. Members of the family who are unable to let the patient go or members of the community who are disturbed at the thought of death may insist that life must be prolonged as long as possible, even if only for a few weeks, no matter what the cost, even if the patient is in great pain and the family may be pauperized in the process. (For example, just to keep a comatose person alive may cost as much as $100,000 a year.) In some states more than others legal restrictions may severely limit medical professionals and caregivers in terms of what they can do.

These dilemmas are pointed up by the American public's insisting on the best of medical care in which every resource is used to prolong life no matter what the cost, while at the same time complaining about the costs of health care.

A More Difficult Problem

So far we have been talking about the refusal of treatment or the withholding of treatment to prolong dying. Now we come to a more difficult and controversial question of whether or not it is ever right to hasten or shorten the period of dying. And this opens up the question of suicide.

Because life can become problematical and increasingly unmanageable for many, suicide has become a major cause of death among the aged, especially among American men in their 80s, most often among men who have been widowed. By way of contrast, in Japan the high suicide rate is among older women, who take this way out from the frustration and shame of having to live as a burden on their children in the household of a daughter-in-law. There is a serious question as to whether many other deaths may be suicides in disguise, or unconscious suicides, consummated by such things as neglecting or refusing to take medicines, exposing the self to accidents, and using drugs, particularly alcohol, to excess. Some of these are impulsive acts of desperation. Others are carefully planned. Older people commit 25% of the suicides, although they constitute only 11% of the population.

In *The Woman Said Yes* Jessamyn West tells how her younger sister, the beautiful and successful one of the family, made a careful and deliberate decision to end her own life when her disability reached a certain point, rather than having the cancer determine when she would die.[7] She wired Jessamyn to come and help her die, meaning to help her live most fully in her final months. Together they planned, making provision for the disposition of her things. They hoarded sleeping pills. They plotted how to circumvent the surveillance of the physician, who, while he may have been sympathetic, was committed by training and ethics to keeping persons alive. When the disease progressed, the sister quietly announced that the time had come. She asked to be dressed in her best nightgown, swallowed the pills, and lay down to the sleep from which she never awoke.

This story is set in the context of the larger story of how their mother had worked to help Jessamyn herself recover from tuberculosis that at that time had seemed incurable. There are, as the book points out, several ways of saying yes to life.

The Giving and Taking of Life

The Judeo-Christian tradition has held that life is a gift from God to be preserved, enhanced, and used in the service of God as a sacred trust. However, it is not life in itself that is primary but the commitment of life to the purposes of God. It is not the length of life but the quality of life that really matters.

So the giving of life in an attempt to save the lives of others or in commitment to a belief or value can become the highest form of sacrifice. Those who sacrifice their lives this way are hailed as the martyrs of the faith or commemorated as heroes or heroines.

It is recognized that life can be risked and often has to be put at risk in the fulfillment of life. Persons are admired for taking high risks in pursuit of adventure or exploration and knowledge. It is not thought reprehensible if persons die while mountain climbing, hang gliding, or sailing across the ocean in a small boat.

While society has affirmed the commandment "Thou shalt not murder," it has thought it right to execute persons regarded as criminals or traitors. To kill in defense of one's own life or the lives of those for whom one is responsible is held to be justified. Our society has not hesitated to draft soldiers and to send them into battle, even recruiting suicide squads or equipping persons with military secrets with the means to kill themselves rather than to reveal the secret.

While the giving of life is one thing, the taking of one's life may be another, although it may be hard to make the distinction between the two. We find the idea of suicide profoundly disturbing, loaded with ambiguity and ambivalence. The threat or the attempt to commit suicide may be a cry for help. It may be an angry gesture with the wish to hurt someone else. It may be an act of desperation when situations have become intolerable and there seems to be no other way out. Or perhaps under some circumstances it may be a rational judgment that life is no longer worth sustaining and that death would remove a burden both from self and others.

After a prolonged discussion a group of scholars representing philosophy, religion, psychiatry, and medicine came to the following conclusion:

> We do not dispute the contention that the majority of suicides represent a rejection of the "gift of life" and, as such, are evidence of severe emotional distress. We believe, however, that a person with a progressive terminal disease faces a unique situation—one which calls for a new look at traditional assumptions about the motivation for choosing suicide. . . .
>
> In our view, this choice might be found to be reasoned, appropriate, altruistic, sacrificial, and loving. We can imagine that an individual faced with debilitating, irreversible illness, who would have to endure intractable pain, mutilating surgery, or demeaning treatments—with added concern for the burden being placed on family and friends—might conclude that suicide was a reasonable, even generous, resolution to a process moving inexorably toward death.[8]

They went on to say that the acceptance of suicide did not mean that they wanted to advocate or encourage it. They oppose institutionalized assistance to persons choosing suicide.

But the conclusions of the scholars quoted above deserve much thought:

> A decision to choose suicide, we believe, should be an independent and private one, made in consultation with family, friends, and trusted health care professionals. If assistance is required to carry out such a decision, we believe it should be provided by those who have an intimate knowledge of the patient and would be acting out of compassion, knowing that the choice had been made voluntarily. We recognize that a request for help in committing suicide may create an acutely painful dilemma for the person who is asked. We do not believe that anyone is ever obligated to assist in suicide.[9]

Those who oppose the withdrawal of life-support systems or the hastening of the process of dying by cessation of medical treatment, and those who oppose suicide, do so because of their respect for the sanctity of life; also they fear to open the door to those who might be inclined to take advantage of this option out of their own self-interest, greed, prejudice, or hatred.

In situations as unprecedented as the one under discussion there will be many different positions taken, all of them fraught with ambiguity and pain. None of them should be taken without prayer.

The Basis for a Decision to Live or Die

Life is precious, even if precarious, a gift from God to cherish and to enhance. We have a vocation to preserve life, to invest it in obedience to God's purposes, and to fulfill it. It belongs to God and is given to us as a trust. To love God is to cherish what he has created and what he cherishes. This includes exercising a stewardship of our own health and doing what we can to live out our life span. Then when the time comes, we give it back to the God who created it.

Because God loves the whole world, we are responsible for preserving and enhancing not only our own lives but also the lives of others to the best of our ability. The lives of others and the life of the human race is of more consequence than any one life. Responsibility for the lives of others includes conservation of the environment in which we live. It includes birth control to keep populations in balance with resources so that the quality of life is optimized. Under some circumstances it may include abortions and the omission of measures to keep badly malformed babies alive. It may involve the sacrifice of life by some that others may live. It may include allowing persons to end their own lives or omitting measures to keep them alive.

The goal is not unending life but eternal life, a quality of life rooted in fellowship with God and in obedience to his will. This is a life of responsibility for self and for others. The responses we make in each situation should be governed by the commitment to love even as Christ loves us, to be willing to suffer for our friends, even to lay down our lives for our friends, if that is what love requires. Love of God and love of the neighbor is the touchstone by which we make our decisions.

Death is an aspect of this existence. Our dying, too, is to be transcended in faith, an offering to God, not as an act in itself but as the culmination of a responsible life well lived. Responsibility to God and to others might mean that we offer this life up for them.

We do not help persons to die, and we do not really plan for our dying. We help others to live as fully as possible in each day given, and we strive to live as responsibly as possible through each day available to us. In one sense each of us is dying, and our lives are terminal. But we do not dwell on that time in the unknown future when life will end. We rejoice now in the gift we have. Neither do we dwell on the past, reliving our mistakes, grieving over lost opportunities or our sins.

Through confession and faith in God's grace the slate is wiped clean each day, so we can make the most of the time given us. To love is to accept the forgiveness that is offered and to live in openness toward the future, which includes our death.

Aging is a progressive loss of the capacity to live, brought on by disease, accident, strain, and atrophy, as well as a running down of the clock built into our genetic structure. It is also a process of becoming fully human, a journey toward the destiny to which we are called. It is the act of playing out our role in the great drama of creation. As we play that role, we participate in the creation of the drama itself, making it what it would not have been except for our participation.

Do we really want to live forever? Would we be able to rectify all our mistakes, find answers to all our questions, and reconcile all our broken relationships if we lived forever? Would we be able to escape boredom? Would there still be challenge and adventure if we were invulnerable? Doubtless immortality would doom us to a relentless succession of repetitive pains as well as satisfactions, to riding the merry-go-round forever rather than making a journey through a land with changing scenery. It would be a disaster for the species.

Death is the final healing of that which is hurt and broken, the renewal of that which is worn out, the completion of that which is only partially finished. That which is imperfect is made whole again in unity with the ground of being out of which it came.

Death makes possible the ongoing creative process. The kernel of wheat dies and loses its individuality when it is placed in the ground. It gains a new individuality when it sprouts. Then fulfilling its function of producing new grains, the stem dies and falls before the reaper's sickle or the weight of the winter snows. Some stalks are broken and destroyed before they produce ears of grain, but they too participate in the process through which God is accomplishing his purposes.

How Then Do We Achieve Our Death?

When our time comes, if it does not come without warning as a complete surprise, we will probably face it as we characteristically face all other new experiences, changes, and separations. As Marjorie Casebier McCoy suggests in her book *To Die with Style,* we all may have our own style of dying, which will be in keeping with our style of living, whether it be accepting, defiant, denying, humorous, tragic, or questing.[10]

But we do have some choices. I can look at death as an interruption, an uprooting, and an exile to some lonely Siberia. If so, I will go reluctantly, resentfully, and unhappily. I can regard it as a command from a superior officer. If so, I will go under orders to some far-off assignment that I did not seek but that I am duty bound to obey, stoically and heroically. I can see it as a commissioning to serve a mission in a different clime and culture. If so, I go with some trepidation but also with some excitement, determined to be faithful to the purpose I serve. Or I can think of it as embarking on an adventure or vacation trip that will expand my horizons and open grand new vistas of knowing.

In her novel *I Heard the Owl Call My Name,* Margaret Craven deals with the naturalness of death as seen from the perspective of the Kwakiutl Indians of British Columbia. A 27-year-old clergyman, Mark Brian, who unknown to him has a terminal illness, is sent as a missionary to the Indians. The bishop who sends him knows that Mark has only a short time to live. Having been a missionary to these people, the bishop believes that Mark might learn from them the meaning of death and so learn to achieve his own death with dignity and grace after fulfilling his own life in ministry.

The life cycle of the salmon which is so closely tied to that of the tribe becomes a central parable. For when their time has come, the mature salmon swim in from the sea and make a dangerous, bruising voyage up the stream to where they were originally hatched. There they deposit their eggs and die. Mark comes to see that

> the whole life of the swimmer is one of courage and adventure. All of it builds to the climax and the end. When the swimmer dies, he has spent himself completely for the end for which he was made and this is not sadness. It is triumph.[11]

It is the wasted life, the life that denies its destiny as a swimmer, that is sad.

In that tribe, when a person knows that death is near he says, "I heard the owl call my name." And no one tries to tell him he was mistaken, because only the one for whom it is intended can hear the call. Mark succumbs to his illness and dies, but not until he has learned the meaning of love, commitment, and identification with those whom he serves. When he dies, an old woman who had become a kind of mother to him repeats a traditional benediction: "Walk straight on, my son. Do not look back. Do not turn your head. You are going to the land of our Lord."[12]

At the end of the book the writer reflects,

> Past the village flowed the river, like time, like life itself, waiting for the swimmer to come again on his way to the climax of his adventurous life, and to the end for which he had been made.[13]

So, if I may change the metaphor, when the time comes to die, like a guest leaving a joyous dinner party organized to celebrate life itself, we put on our coats, thank our Host, step out into the night, close the door behind us, and go to our own house, where we will sleep safely, wrapped in the love from which nothing can separate us, having done all that was given us to do.

Notes

Chapter One: New Images of Old Age

1. May Sarton, *At Seventy: A Journal* (New York: W. W. Norton, 1984), p. 13.
2. Ronald Blythe, *The View in Winter: Reflections on Old Age* (New York: Penguin, 1979).
3. *The Myth and Reality of Aging in America* (Washington, D. C.: National Council on the Aging, 1975).
4. Abraham J. Heschel, "The Older Person in the Perspective of Jewish Tradition," in *Aging and the Human Spirit: A Reader in Religion and Gerontology,* ed. Carol LeFevre and Perry LeFevre (Chicago: Exploration Press, 1981), p. 39.
5. John A. B. MacLeish, *The Ulyssean Adult: Creativity in the Middle and Late Years* (New York: McGraw-Hill, 1976).
6. *The Kansas City Times,* May 2, 1984. Section A-3.
7. James F. Fries and Laurance Crapo, *Vitality and Aging: Implications of the Rectangular Curve* (San Francisco: W. H. Freeman and Company, 1981).
8. *The Poetic and Dramatic Works of Alfred Tennyson* (Boston: Houghton Mifflin, 1898), p. 87.

Chapter Two: Living through Transitions

1. Albert Lansing, "General Biology of Senescence," in *Handbook of Aging and the Individual: Psychological and Biological Aspects*, ed. James Birren (Chicago: University of Chicago Press, 1959), p. 119.
2. H. Tristram Engelhardt, "Is Aging a Disease?" in *Life Span*, ed. Robert M. Veatch (New York: Harper & Row, 1979), p. 180.
3. Daniel Yankelovich, *New Rules: Searching for Self-Fulfillment in a World Turned Upside Down* (New York: Bantam Books, 1982).
4. Peter Marris, *Loss and Change* (New York: Pantheon, 1974).

Chapter Three: Saying Amen to All of Life

1. Blythe, *View in Winter.*
2. Robert Butler, *Why Survive? Being Old in America* (New York: Harper & Row, 1975).
3. Isaac Bashevis Singer, *The Penitent* (New York: Farrar, Straus, & Giroux, 1983), p. 168.
4. Lisle Marburg Goodman, *Los Angeles Times,* September 8, 1975. Part 2, pp. 1-5.
5. Paul Tournier, *Learn to Grow Old* (New York: Harper & Row, 1971).
6. Rubem Alves, *A Theology of Human Hope* (New York: Corpus Books, 1969), pp. 139-140.
7. Robert Coles, *The Old Ones of New Mexico* (New York: Doubleday, 1975).
8. Antoine de Saint-Exupery, *Wind, Sand, and Stars* (New York: Harcourt Brace Jovanovich, 1967).
9. Heschel, p. 42.
10. A. R. Hochschild, *The Unexpected Community* (Englewood Cliffs, N.J.: Prentice-Hall, 1973).

Chapter Four: Singing at Midnight

1. Langdon Gilkey, *Maker of Heaven and Earth* (New York: Doubleday, 1959), p. 179.
2. Reinhold Niebuhr, *Nature and Destiny of Man* (New York: Scribner's, 1949).

3. John Macquarrie, *Principles of Christian Theology* (New York: Scribner's, 1966), pp. 232-237.

4. Bernhard Anderson, *Creation and Chaos: The Reinterpretation of Mythical Symbolism in the Bible* (New York: Association Press, 1967).

5. James Russell Lowell, "The Present Crisis" in *The Vision of Sir Launfal and Other Poems* (Boston: Houghton Mifflin, 1905).

6. Robert Ingersoll, *The Works of Robert Ingersoll,* ed. Clinton P. Farrell, 12 vols. (New York: Dresden Publishing Co., 1902). Quoted in Orvin Larson, *American Infidel: Robert Ingersol, A Biography* (Secaucus, N.J.: Citadel Press, 1968), p. 142.

7. Nikos Kazantzakis, *Zorba the Greek* (New York: Ballantine Books, 1952).

8. Sally Godow, "Frailty and Strength: The Dialectic in Aging," *The Gerontologist,* 23.2 (April 1983), p. 146.

Chapter Five: Listen to Your Calling

1. Viktor Frankl, *Man's Search for Meaning* (Boston: Beacon, 1962).

2. Bronislaw Malinowski, *Argonatus of the Western Pacific* (New York: E. P. Dutton, 1922).

3. Evelyn M. Berger, *This One Thing I Do* (Lima, Ohio: CSS, 1984).

4. H. Richard Niebuhr, *The Purpose of the Church and Its Ministry* (New York: Harper and Brothers, 1956).

5. Frankl, *Man's Search.*

Chapter Six: Inherit the Kingdom

1. Cf. the article on "Life" by O. A. Piper in *The Interpreter's Dictionary of the Bible,* vol. 3 (Nashville: Abingdon, 1962), pp. 124-130. See also C. H. Dodd, *The Interpretation of the Fourth Gospel* (New York: Cambridge University Press, 1953), pp. 144-150.

2. Alan Richardson, "Salvation, Savior," *The Interpreter's Dictionary of the Bible,* vol. 4 (Nashville: Abingdon, 1962), p. 168.

3. *Aging in America: Trials and Triumphs* (Monticello, Ill.: Americana Health Care Coporation, 1980).
4. Abraham Maslow, *Motivation and Personality* (New York: Harper & Row, 1954).
5. Leo Simmons, *The Role of the Aged in Primitive Society* (New Haven, Conn.: Yale University Press, 1945).
6. Erik Erikson, "Identity and the Life Cycle," *Psychological Issues* 1, no. 1 (1959).
7. Robert Peck, "Psychological Developments in the Second Half of Life," in *Psychological Aspects of Aging,* ed. John E. Anderson (Washington, D.C.: American Psychological Association, 1956).
8. I am indebted to Sister Terrie Ann Lewis, chaplain at Prairie View Mental Health Center in Newton, Kansas, for suggesting this list of tasks for the later years, which I have adapted.
9. Florida Scott-Maxwell, *The Measure of My Days* (New York: Knopf, 1968), p. 42.
10. Loren Eisley, *The Immense Journey* (New York: Random House, 1959).
11. Ibid., p. 12.

Chapter Seven: Live under the Rainbow

1. Erich Fromm, *The Revolution of Hope: Toward a Humanized Technology* (New York, Harper & Row, 1968), cf. p. 9 ff.
2. Marjorie Lowenthal et al., *Four Stages of Life* (San Francisco: Jossey-Bass, 1975), pp. 122ff.
3. Robert Carrigan, "Where Has Hope Gone? Toward An Understanding of Hope in Pastoral Care," *Pastoral Psychology,* 25:no. 1 (Fall 1976), p. 43.
4. Ibid., p. 52.
5. John Macquarrie, *Christian Hope* (New York: Seabury, 1978), p. 28.
6. Frankl, *Man's Search.*
7. Norman Young, "What Hope Is There?" *The Drew Getaway* (Madison, N.J.: Theological School, Drew University, 1975-76), p. 40

8. David C. Clemans, *God with Us.* Printed privately. pp. 37-38.

Chapter Eight: A Time to Die

1. Philippe Aries, *The Hour of Our Death* (New York: Knopf, 1981).
2. Herman Feifel, ed., *New Meanings of Death* (New York: McGraw-Hill, 1977), p. 4.
3. A. Roy Eckhardt, "Death in the Judaic and Christian Traditions," in *Death in American Experience,* ed. Aren Mack (New York: Schocken, 1973).
4. Quoted in Eckhardt.
5. Florida Scott-Maxwell, *Measure of My Days.*
6. Louis S. Baer, *Let the Patient Decide: A Doctor's Advice to Older Persons* (Philadelphia: Westminster, 1978).
7. Jessamyn West, *The Woman Said Yes* (New York: Harcourt Brace Jovanovich, 1976).
8. "Suicide for the Terminally Ill: A Need for New Thinking," *Concern for Dying* 6, no. 4 (Fall 1980), p. 4.
9. Ibid.
10. Marjorie Casebier McCoy, *To Die with Style* (Nashville: Abingdon, 1974).
11. Margaret Craven, *I Heard the Owl Call My Name* (New York: Doubleday, 1973), p. 39.
12. Ibid., p. 148.
13. Ibid.